ANGRY WAITERS

HAPPY BIRTHDAY
AKIKO SAN !

Felici

Happy
Reads
Rel

Boldog
Szülétésnapot

Beatrix

Happy Birthday
Yuzo

ANGRY WAITERS

Survival on a cruise ship

Federico Fumagalli

2nd Edition – Extra Anger!

Copyright © 2013, 2020 by Federico Fumagalli
Photographs Copyright © 2020
by Federico Fumagalli
Front and back cover Copyright © 2013, 2020
by Federico Fumagalli

Cover design by Associated Digital

All rights reserved. No part of this publication may be reproduced, distributed, or transmitted in any form or by any means, including photocopying, recording, or other electronic or mechanical methods, without the prior written permission of the author, except in the case of brief quotations for certain non-commercial uses permitted by copyright law. For permission requests, the author can be contacted by email angry@federicofumagalli.com

First Edition 2013
Second Edition 2020

ISBN: 9798639921513

For more books from Federico Fumagalli
www.federicofumagalli.com

THANKS TO:

Timothy Langton
for helping me to create this book;
Mauro Rota and Andrea Ratti of Operathing
for the front cover picture.

This book is dedicated to all the waiters, runners and
servers of this planet, and of other planets as well;
it is also dedicated to my wife for love and patience;
to my son, to whom I wish to steer away from this
career;
my family;
my friends and colleagues.

viii

CONTENTS OF TERROR

1~ FASTEN YOUR SEAT BELT 1
2~ IT'S FULL OF AMERICANS 10
3~ JANUARY 18th, SATURDAY: Maybe too early in the morning 18
4~ LOST IN BRATA 31
5~ DAY 2 41
6~ BASIC SHI(F)TS 46
7~ DONATELLO DINING ROOM 56
8~ CANALETTO DINING ROOM 60
9~ THE BAKED ALASKA 65
10~ LIDO BREAKFAST 67
11~ LIDO LUNCH 110
12~ FREE SUNDAE 114
13~ NAPKIN FOLDING 123
14~ ISLAND NIGHT 125
15~ CHAMPAGNE WATERFALL 127
16~ DAUGHTER OF THE QUEEN CAYS: The Neverland 135
17~ WAR OF THE WORLDS 140
18~ THE ~~DYING ROOM~~ DINING ROOM SHIFT: wHELLcome 147
19~ BREAKFAST IN HELL 155
20~ LUNCH 164
21~ THE LOBSTER: Gala dinner 170
22~ THE GALLEY ROUND 181
23~ WINE TASTING AND TIME WASTING 202
24~ TEATIME 204
25~ IN PORT MANNING AND SEXUAL EMBARRASSMENT 210
26~ TIPS 217
27~ THAT NIGHT WHEN I WAS SO DRUNK THAT I CAN'T REMEMBER
    ANYTHING AT ALL 227
28~ DO NOT TOUCH MY ICE CREAM 228
29~ THE CONQUEST OF SAINT MARTIN 235
30~ SAINT THOMAS 243
31~ SALARY ON THE SEABED 249
32~ MISSION IMPUSSYBLE 253
33~ FORT LAUDERDALE AND MIAMI 268
34~ USPH: We are under attack 274
35~ THE BEAUTY IN RED 279
36~ LAST DAY 289
37~ EPILOGUE 300
38~ GLOSSARY 302

x

~~1~~
FASTEN YOUR SEAT BELT

After a sleepless night, at exactly 04.00am, I stretch my hands towards the ceiling of my room yawning big time. I'm already nervous and upset: I hate having to get up so early, especially if I haven't been able to fall asleep.

In Italy, Friday the 17th, is like Friday the 13th in Britain. So, this doesn't look like a lucky day; I can see it written in my Pan di Stelle cookies (literally Bread of Stars, chocolate brown cookies with white glazed stars on top), from which the lucky stars have disappeared. Only the brown is left, which is not a good omen colour.

I reach Malpensa airport in Milan and I say farewell to my Peugeot 206 and my parents, and as I arrive I don't know how to get around a closed 'Information Service' and a not yet open 'Ticket Office'. I know nothing of airports, except of course that aircrafts take off, land, and sometimes crash.

After a few minutes for getting accustomed to the surroundings, I roam between millions of indications in a labyrinth of codes and signs towards an unknown end. I check and recheck my flight ticket, worried about forgetting its code. I know worrying is useless, but the destiny I've seen on my Pan di Stelle speaks clear: worry.

But then I take off for Zurich, and one hour later is

Angry Waiters   *Federico Fumagalli*

still the cold to hit me when I need to change airplane. I follow the signs and I reach the 'Pre-embarkation' desk, when after twenty minutes of queue the check-in girl tells me to go back to the 'Immigration' desk because I skipped it. I join the queue at Immigration, I rejoin the queue at Embarkation, and with a dumb smile on my face – one of the last smiles ☺ for the next few months – I proceed and grab my *34A Window* seat that will have to bear my presence for ten hours.

As soon as I sit down I fasten my seatbelt and, once my neighbour has taken his seat two places over to my right, I start fooling around.

This is the second time that I have got onto an airplane: the first time was a year before, but my friend and I were probably too drunk to remember how we got on board and what happened before and during the flight. More importantly: what happened in Ibiza.

I unfasten my seatbelt – the aircraft hasn't taken off yet – and I ask my neighbour to move and let me go to the young Steward to ask him if I can listen to my CD player. He tells me that I must wait until we are high in the sky, like near the moon, and the signal 'Fasten your Seatbelt' turns off. In his opinion it could be dangerous using electronic devices during 'take off' and 'landing' phases, though I couldn't give a damn of his opinion.

I go back to my seat giving trouble to my neighbour, but before he gets the chance to sit back, I kindly ask him to wait a moment: I need to pick up my CDs and CD player from my hand luggage located up in the bag compartment. At the time of my embarkation there were not such things like iPods, MP3 players, iPhones... and if there were any, I didn't know what they were. The coolest gadget was a CD player with an anti-shock system.

After two minutes of standing up, he tries to sit, but I stop him and make him stand up again: I'm done, and I need to pass and grab my window seat.

Waiting for the aircraft to take off, I decide to look around the people, only to realise that there's nothing to do but scanning the cute hostesses who walk back and forth. Suddenly, I remember that my ticket is *totally free*, I didn't have to pay for it, reason why I think it's worth it to take wild advantage of whatever they're going to offer.

The first hostess brings a blue blanket, which is wrapped like a T-shirt, so I think I can take it away later as a gift.

Sorry, dreamer: the blanket stays on board.

Then I show off my natural intuitive abilities in mistaking music connection earphones with TV and Radio, so I'm struggling to change the TV channel and volume without realising that I'm still on Radio channel. With an in-need-of-somebody puppy's look on my face I search for a hostess, which, quicker than myself, understands the problem and explains me to plug in the double-plug earphone supplied by the airline, and not *mine*.

It doesn't matter anyway, I've got my CD player: I

can't wait to be side by side with the moon to switch it on.

Eventually the aircraft takes off and I put my nose on the window watching the landscape quickly disappearing backwards. When finally the airplane stabilises itself mid-air, the sun reveals powerful enough to burn me with rage, and I turn annoying to my neighbour again because I need to take sunglasses from my bag. When I sit back by the window I discover a small panel that I can easily pull down without any danger. Fair enough, I don't need sunglasses.

Shortly after, the show of hostesses and stewards distributing chocolates and candies begins: since I didn't have to pay for the ticket, I try to grab whatever they have got.

Arrival time is scheduled for 21.30.

While I listen to a Blind Guardian's CD I make an attempt to take a nap, but the blond hostess *with* the ponytail almost leaves me with an empty stomach: I call her back immediately, begging her to refill my mignon tray with everything she can manage to put on it, including a hot tea and a small bottle of white wine that causes me drowsiness for an hour.

When I wake up I feel even drowsier than before, so I decide to call again the blond hostess *with* the ponytail to get me another tea for a mind and body revival. Waiting for the drink to make a full recovery on my mind and body, I take a look at the five magazines purposefully badly positioned down in the seat, in front of my legs: one of these reports all the movies that will be shown later on.

I can't make a decision: how about a movie where a classic American family has many problems like a cow that refuses to be milked? Why the hell do a classic American family need a cow?

How about a Chinese thriller with Thai subtitles?

No way...

The hours really pass by so slowly that I'm bored to death. I can't even sleep; a little bit because Blind Guardian doesn't play relaxing music, a little bit because my seat is just beside the left wing's engine. I don't even want to try and talk to my male neighbour: if he was a young pretty lady, I wouldn't lose the chance to show her how poor I am at flirting on an airplane.

While my sluggishness is about to take over, giving moments of sweet sleepiness, the hostesses and stewards come back to attack: their job now is to dispatch the Immigration Documents to fill in before landing. They come written in thirty languages, except for Italian.

So, to keep out of boredom, I decide that I don't feel like filling them in myself, urging assistance from one of those talented hostesses. I keep in mind that I got the ticket for free, so I'm more than pleased to be a pain in the ass.

Here she comes, the blond hostess *without* ponytail, asking me something regarding my Visa on the

Angry Waiters *Federico Fumagalli*

passport because I should stay in USA territory for a few months due to job conditions. I pretend not to understand a word of English, and she asks me if I speak German – even worse – but facing my very negative answer and my very scared face, she suddenly becomes Spanish. I look at her terrorised.

Surprisingly my neighbour comes in play with an attempt of I-Thai-lian conversation, but the attempt crumbles down the valley.

Next to our seats there is a lady who's curiously looking at the scene, and her look seems to get more thoughtful when I declare to my hostess that I'm about to embark on a prestigious cruise liner with the position of Junior Waiter, also called the Runner, but better known as the Slave. The lady looks at me as if I am crazy and wakes her husband up who, after a very unwilling glance at me, he gives her a 'fuck-off-for-waking-me-up' evil eye and curls himself down again.

The 'Battle for the Immigration Documents' isn't over yet: my hostess tells me that she will be in charge of filling them up for me, or she will smash a mignon tray on my forehead. I speak, she writes. Work completed I check the papers, I pass them into her cured hands and she shows a triumphant smile. She can now get rid of me.

I just have a few doubts about a few questions:

– Are you bringing with you more than ten thousand dollars? (If I had them I wouldn't go to work on a cruise ship).

Angry Waiters   *Federico Fumagalli*

– Are you coming in under the intention of accomplishing terrorist acts, violence, theft, traffic of illegal products, *religious colonisation*? Or have you ever been charged for taking part in one or more of those activities?

I am really tempted to answer 'YES' to every question, but I don't want to be jailed so young. After having explained to my Thai neighbour that I'm not going on a cruise ship for a romantic holiday, but to work like a donkey, I call back the blonde hostess *with* the ponytail for another complimentary tea.

Business done I need to change music, but Children of Bodom's Hatebreeder is still in my CD bag in the bag compartment: I have to stand up, being a pain in the ass once more with my neighbour, who is gradually becoming a very pissed off neighbour and decides to change seat. Great: I now have three seats all for me.

After a while it's dinner time, but time seems to be standing still, it's not passing by, really, I'm getting nervous, the ten hour flight seems infinite given that I must stay in my dog-seat with no chance of moving. Despite the fact that I keep the seatbelt on all the time, I don't feel so safe on an airplane; if we crash – as it will probably happen sooner or later – at least I can say 'my seatbelt was fastened!', though having the seatbelt on is not synonym of survival if the airplane crashes into a banana field.

Boredom, boredom, boredom, even with death metal playing in my earphones, nothing happens and...

Angry Waiters   *Federico Fumagalli*

...hey... no...

what's that...?

An hour before landing something happens: a sensational turbulence shakes the aircraft like milkshake in a blender. I check that my seatbelt is well locked, I even tie it up some more, we are all going to die and I am the only one with the seatbelt on (not that it would make any difference when we crash, but it's time to find out): feels like being on a roller-coaster, adrenaline and danger included in the ticket, people who scream, kids that cry, seats off their hinges and flying mignon trays...

But just like all the nice dreams, everything comes to an end – I mean the turbulence – and when the aircraft gets back in place I look at the brave passengers queuing at the bathroom to throw up.

Some of them can't wait, and despite pressing both hands on their mouth, they spill vomit on the floor. Hostesses and stewards go crazy to clean up, but the flight that the Captain wished us to be pleasant is not pleasant any more: the smell is unbearable.

After that the blonde hostess *with* the ponytail passes around to give fabulous boiling wet serviettes to clean face and hands.

We are now about to ~~crash~~ land: I understand we are landing because my ears are blocking up slowly slowly, painfully painfully. My hearing is diminishing, and the solution to all my problems is to close my nostrils with two fingers and blow. My ears uncap like

Angry Waiters *Federico Fumagalli*

a Crodino and I come back to the world of noise (Crodino is a famous Italian aperitif; in the TV adverts they say 'Stappa un Crodino!' – 'Uncap a Crodino!').

Slowly, I'm landing. Scanning the landscape I can see Miami airport, Florida. It's surrounded by the Atlantic Ocean.

The wheels touch the ground as if there was a pillow on the landing lane and then a general applause follows.

We haven't crashed after all, so I haven't been able to test the seatbelts.

I take my winter clothes off (in Malpensa airport it was zero degrees Celsius) because here it feels quite hot. Today, Friday the 17th, I land in America, and it's only the beginning of the end.

My G-Shock tells me that '*It's 21.30 and you are in big troubles*', but here it's just 15.30. Still a long way to go before the end of this unlucky day.

With an idiotic look on my face I say bye-bye to the crew, especially to the two blonde hostesses *with* and *without* ponytail; I think what I have metaphorically left behind me and I imagine what I will find. But I want to be optimistic this time, and with a big '…Vaffanculo…' I go to collect my bags.

~~2~~
IT'S FULL OF AMERICANS

America is full of Americans. Or so I was told. By the look of the people around me, the only Americans are the Security Officers, the Police, and the couple right in front of me in the queue who are french kissing without mercy, making me feel a bit uncomfortable because I don't know where to look to avoid watching them. Can't they wait to arrive in the hotel room?

This is one of those awkward moments where you wish for a quick death: if I stare at them I might look like a maniac. If I look around, I might look like an idiot anyway.

Wish I could simply headbutt them.

The problem with the Americans is that now I have to get used to them. Or them to me.

It's no more like at home, because from now on I'm in a very foreign land and English is the only language I should be aware of. Since I'm not a black belt of English, it's about time to test my ability in *not* understanding what people *says*.

And here all my problems begin.

I easily pass through custom and border control with success, I wait for the Custom's Officers to reassure themselves that the most dangerous weapon I'm carrying is a *nail clipper*, then I find the small man with the big sign in his hands showing the name of the cruise liner. There I meet with three Rumanians (from

Romania, I guess): Ciprian, Mihiai and Monika.

We get out of the waiting area to wait for the Crew Bus, and I try to get hold of my mythological old mobile phone, about the size of a pineapple, just to find there is no signal. Not the slightest hint of it. I can only put back the time six hours.

Here comes the Crew Bus, and from now on I take note of American's habits and customs: first of all there's the exaggeration mania, the tendency to the new and cool, and then the attention seeking. Americans *must* make themselves noticed, not only by foreigners: among themselves too.

The Crew Bus is questionably painted with all sort of colours; looks like somebody dropped a shelf of phosphorescent wall paint cans on it. On the side door there's 'Comfort Inn Hotel' written, but I hardly believe it to be 'Comfort'. And even less 'Hotel'. Maybe not even 'Inn'.

The radio is set on the highest volume, but at least it's tuned in to an unlistenable Mexican channel; the Communication Radio for Information and Direction Centre is on hands-free mode. A wicked voice occasionally sparks up as if possessed by devil; also the Driver screams through the microphone like a Captain in command of a Traffic Battalion: 'Andale! Andale!' mixed with horn beating is how I guess he can move cars out of his way.

As if it wasn't enough, the engine's rumble sounds more like the one of a Formula One racing car at the

Angry Waiters   *Federico Fumagalli*

near point of exploding. Maybe that's the reason why the radio is so loud, or is it the consequence?

Another amazing thing is the horn: if you think in Milan it's annoying the sound of hundreds of horns that play harmoniously like a Black Metal band, listen to this one and you will change idea. This Crew Bus's horn has the power of six thunders and a wave length of a typhoon. It would shatter a shop of unbreakable glasses, and that's the reason why the Crew Bus doesn't have any windows. Or, more likely, it had them before.

The Driver considers this as the new weapon against his Urban Traffic Battles: the louder the horn, the quicker you go. Even ambulances stop to let him through.

In America everyone has his own cognition of priority: they overtake on each side, even climbing on the roof of the car in front of them if necessary, and if one dares to raise the middle finger, a horn's beat is more than enough to clear the ideas.

The fact that traffic lights are red or green or multicolour is optional: if green, they push their foot down to get priority; if yellow, they push their foot down because their priority is tiny, but still *theirs*; if red, they start to hit the horn before pushing their foot down again because... they always must have priority.

Nobody wants to stop, and Mr Driver seems to be a fond patriot; he doesn't want to stop either. I understand this when, taking the last long straight that

Angry Waiters   *Federico Fumagalli*

should bring us *alive* to the Comfort Inn Hotel, he is still travelling at the approximate speed of one hundred and twenty km/h and we are twenty metres away from the Hotel's car park. Only at the last moment I realise that the Crew Bus doesn't have brakes: instead, the Driver furiously grabs the handbrake with *both* hands leaving the wheel to its own destiny, and he marvels a legendary move pulling the damn handbrake towards his chest grinning his teeth, and while my life passes by with bells and horns, I can't stop wondering about the Driver's ability who, with his sight still on the handbrake, pulls a hand on the steering wheel turning it three hundred and sixty degrees and I feel the Crew Bus spinning toward the Hotel's entrance, suddenly stopping with smoking tyres against a small brick wall. I thought I was going to die in an airplane crash, but just because it didn't happen it does not mean that I have to die on a Crew Bus.

Jumping down the bus I hear the tyres yelling 'We made it!' and I kiss the ground, then I enter the hotel sitting in the hall, on one of those very still and soft armchairs to gain some colour back on my face, happy that my underwear hasn't turned the colour of my Pan di Stelle.

Room keys are given out to everybody and I run to take possession of mine: a double room with two double beds all for me. Maybe America is not that bad.

Or is this just an illusion?

As I enter I am welcomed by a couple of penguins

Angry Waiters   *Federico Fumagalli*

who show me the way; the two double beds have four layers of blankets five centimetres thick each. Americans don't care about the outside temperature: what they want is a difference of fifteen degrees Celsius less inside. I switch off the air conditioning and I try to open the window, but every effort is vain because it's been sealed. I can't open it. Why?! Because I shouldn't be in need of a window: there's the air conditioner!

The real reason why windows over the 3rd floor are sealed is to prevent people from committing suicide jumping out of them. It's not a matter of being sensitive towards people: a person who killed himself would be a terrible publicity for the hotel.

Before dinner I take a shower, and I must admit the geniality of these people: the shower sprinkler, for example, gives me twelve different water sprays, simply by turning the lever. Why the hell do they need twelve of them?

Willing to avoid trouble I choose 'Soft Shower', which shoots water with the pressure of one hundred and fifty atmosphere and I'm scared of being pierced from side to side. I have to tie myself with a double rope not to be swept away.

I'm surprised to see that the sprinkler can only spit water with an angle of sixty degrees and I can turn it only left and right but not up and down. Indeed, as I get nearer to adjust its water flow in order to avoid dismembering my face, by mistake I turn the lever in

Angry Waiters   *Federico Fumagalli*

the wrong way, and the new selection brings me to taste the power of a hurricane that promises me a reinvigorating body work – or whatever will be left of my body. I couldn't see it, but on the last two levers there is "Strong Body Massage" and "Chuck Norris Body Massage".

Desperately I look for a lifebelt – of which there's no trace – but I can only bravely cling on to a towel and I am safe. At least: for now.

Drying up my befogged mirror I look at my outcast expression: WTF?!

Then as usual I dry myself, I comb my hair, I put on some hair gel and finally I remember that first of all I should have dressed up. So I dress up, I re-comb my hair, I re-gel, and then I decide to face the hair dryer: its innocent look betrays me: it blows six hundred megatons.

And me, double idiot: I just gelled my hair twice, do I really need to dry them?

After the bathroom adventure I meet my new roommate: Mr Cucu; another Rumanian.

I go back to sit on the soft blankets, but my butt is just half a metre from them when the door is knocked again: the previous trio of Rumanians come to collect me and Cucu for dinner.

We walk down the stairs, and even before the end I recognise the face of the lady on the airplane, the one who woke up her husband and got a good word for that.

The Fantastic Four and I go to seat beside them; it

seems that they know each other: indeed, they worked together on other cruises, but the couple is from Poland.

At the table we wait to be served, just to realise after twenty minutes that we have to move our hungry stomachs toward the counter and place our order there.

After a couple of eternities here it comes: what I ordered looks like nothing I have ever seen before and tastes like sick owl.

I gulp down this clay-looking thing, I say goodnight to my new friends and future colleagues, and I go back to my room. I sneak under four layers of thick blankets and try to sleep, given that for me is 03.00, but here is just 21.00.

I'm about to enter the magic world of erotic dreams when Cucu enters the room and switches the lights on. He asks me if I'm sleeping. I answer "Yes".

For that he gets hold of the remote control and respective TV, changing all of the three hundred and fifty channels on a desperate search for late porn, that doesn't happen to show up unless he pays.

Thanks god he doesn't.

I want to sleep, so I moan kindly to let him know that 'I have had enough for today!' but as if that wasn't enough, in two minutes time the other trio of Rumanians knock at the door. Very well! Welcome everybody!

They chat and laugh until midnight – 06.00 for my body's jet lag – and eventually I hope that they would get their asses out of the way.

Wrong. They want to stay and chat again. Another half an hour.

From the bottom of my heart I wish the window wasn't sealed, and I could throw them all out.

Finally they decide to disappear.

I declare the end of my very long Friday 17th.

I can finally Rest In Peace.

Angry Waiters   *Federico Fumagalli*

~~3~~
JANUARY 18th, SATURDAY:
Maybe too early in the morning

My angry G-Shock alarm wakes me up as if it was upset with me, so I have to get up at 06.30 for a shower and shave, maybe have breakfast, and at 07.00 the Crew Bus is still there waiting for us: the Driver looks drunk and torn, same as yesterday, and his job is to bring the happy Crew from the Comfort Inn to our ship, possibly alive, where we can finally start our six months of hard work.

Mr Driver enters the motorway feeding the tollgate with a couple of coins, while I spend my time watching people at the wheel of their cars. I take a mental note of their scary way to overtake and their dangerous manoeuvres which remind me of the Chinese driving style; only, here cars are bigger and faster. Americans are greedy for road danger.

The first destroyed car is brown, and not only the left side tires are missing, but also the door's paint has left a good twenty metre long mark on the safety wall that divides the two roads.

The second car crash has been quite violent: there is a Chevrolet stuck in the right door of a small bus, like the one I'm sitting on now, and the episode is surrounded by policemen wandering everywhere.

The Crew Bus gets off the motorway and I learn

something: for Americans, car crashes are a big show. Passing by a traffic light embedded in a vehicle who tried to challenge it, I hear the people's comments, and the fact that the Fire Brigade is there to stop the fire, for them is exciting.

When something disastrous happens, the more pyrotechnic it is, the more likely it is to shake their adrenaline emotion, capable of beating the human wave of any Italian stadium when Italy wins the World Cup.

After this trip where the Crew Bus's brakes seem to work properly – I don't know how and why – I arrive to Fort Lauderdale, whose port name is Port Everglades, and I remain impressed by the massive structure and size of the ship that's waiting for me with regal indifference.

The ship I'm going up to can welcome two thousand eight hundred Passengers, plus one thousand two hundred Crew. It's my first cruise – working cruise – and this is one of the biggest and most luxurious in the world. I can't write the name of the company otherwise they would sue me, but I can give you a hint which may or may not lead you to its true name: its name in English could be a similar equivalent to the regal title of "Daughter of the Queen", while the ship itself could be named after the colour of the sand of any exotic beach, or anything that has been coloured with gold.

Hence, I am on board the "Daughter Of The Queen Coloured In Gold (DOTQCIG)"

Angry Waiters Federico Fumagalli

The DOTQCIG has a tonnage of about one hundred and nine thousand tons. I wonder how many of 'me' it would take to make its weight, considering that I'm just fifty kilograms: my mind races through mathematical labyrinths that I never learnt at school, but here you go: there should be twenty-one million eight hundred thousand 'me'.

Truth is, this is an approximate calculation: my weight at the moment of my embarkation is forty-nine Kg. The required minimum weight to work is fifty Kg, which means that I have been employed *illegally,* asking the doctor to falsify my medical report by adding one kilo.

"I add one kilo, but you promise me to eat more, OK?"

He said to me a few weeks earlier.

"Please feel free to buy yourself two bananas: the other one you can eat it." I wanted to reply to him, though I didn't.

Instead, I said: "No problem my friend".

My medical report is the following: No consolidation (*of what?*). Noticed residual mild bilateral hilar sclerosis. Normal hemi diaphragm, normal costofrenic angles.

I still don't know if it's positive or not.

The ship is seventeen decks tall, and if I look at the top from where I am for too long, my neck becomes stiff.

As I get on board I'm hammered with confusion:

Angry Waiters   *Federico Fumagalli*

hundreds of entrances and exits, corridors, staircases, steps, small service lifts, big service lifts, halls, rooms, herds of people... I must follow the mass if I don't want to get lost; I come to the 'Crew Bar', the meeting point for the Crew whenever they have time off. My superiors hand me down heaps of documents coming out of their gun machines, including: a postcard; a magnetic room key for my cabin 3329; the 'Crew Card' for our personal beverage; the 'Credo', which is a Ten Rules card containing the basic rules to follow if we want to pride ourselves of being called 'DOTQCIG Members'. In addition to those Ten Rules there are hundreds more, and I begin to curl my nose like a spider pretending to be dead: too many rules for me.

After the chaotic routine I am brought to 'Canaletto Restaurant', where my end begins. Head Waiters make the general roll call followed by a quick chat with the Maître d'; then the Supervisors introduce themselves as the most *cooperative* people ever, and one of them is someone I met years before in Italy. He didn't expect to find me there, and neither did I. He tells me that there are other Italians on board, just a few, although this does not necessarily mean to be good news.

Thereafter, Robert S, a Polish Waiter, leads me along a tortuous labyrinth bristling with traps which ends in the 'Laundry', where I'm flooded with a high tide of uniforms: black trousers, beige Bermuda shorts, green flowery shirts, two kinds of white shirt – one with vertical stripes and one plain – black vest, green vest,

Angry Waiters   *Federico Fumagalli*

white neckless jacket with white and blue stripes on the top of the sleeves, black bow tie, American theme bow tie, French theme bow tie, Italian theme bow tie, large belt with matching colours of bow tie, buttons that I have to take off from one jacket before wearing another – what a pain in the arse – name badge with nationality and qualification. Mine says 'Frederico – Junior Waiter – Italy', which is wrong.

They added an 'R', as if they wanted to welcome me by giving me an extra letter. Or maybe they thought I was deficient enough not to know how to write my own name.

Later on I would notify one of my many supervisors explaining to him in detail that on my name badge there is an extra 'R' that should be taken off.

After one week I receive another badge: my new name is now *FREDEICO*. Those mentally retarded people have taken the wrong 'R' off, and the badge goes straight into the bin with an accuracy that basketball players would dream of.

I decide to keep the first wrong one, and this is how from today I am completely a new person, a new *ME:* I am officially Mr Frederico, no more Mr Federico.

Then Robert brings me all the way along to my cabin 3329, suggesting to me what kind of uniform I need to wear later on, in which dining room I should go and most importantly: at what time. As soon as he walks out of my micro-cabin, I'm assaulted with fear: how am I supposed to remember the way to whatever

Angry Waiters   *Federico Fumagalli*

Dining Room it was?

The main problem is that I have to dress up quickly. First of all I swear to the cabin's honour, whose volume must have diminished with time.

This is not a cabin; it's a double coffin – but not double size: double stands for 'two people' – with the bathroom in common sharing with two Thai guys in the room opposite ours. The bathroom has the size of an Easter Chocolate Egg, whose surprise is the mignon shower which seems to have a normal sprinkle with only one type of waterfall; drop by drop, slowly, slowly. Just... one one.

For the ones who suffer with claustrophobia, this is the perfect place to keep suffering.

Coming back into the room the space seems three times wider, even though I can hardly walk inside it. Between the mirror and my closet I can't really spread out my arms completely, and if I take a better look under the mirror I can see...

...Hey! What's that?! A cappuccino cup? What the hell is it doing in my cabin...? No, no, just a moment: that's not a cappuccino cup, that's my *washing sink*!! Am I supposed to wash my ugly face with that? I bet even Barbie would have trouble, so small it is.

In my room there is another Polish guy, Robert M, who sleeps on top of the bunk bed; I have to take the bed below. I can't even sit with my back straight up otherwise I bang my head on his butt, which is no fun for neither of us.

Angry Waiters   *Federico Fumagalli*

There are both American and European plug sockets, so I can charge my pineapple-sized phone -the one I brought from Italy- that here doesn't work, except for the alarm.

My bed and my drawer look like battlefields, given that the wild Crusader that stayed before me is gone leaving all his possessions there for me. His smelly pyjamas are half way out of the white pillow, which is yellow in the middle where once there was his dirty head. I can't image the inside of the bed sheets, but I can guess their condition. And who is gonna change them?

In the evening explanations will be given to me about changing sheets and the Crypt's cleaning even without Holy Water, because on the ship everything is a business, and everybody is on board only and solely for money. Caring for Passengers? Are you kidding me?

Robert suggests me not to wash the bedding:

"Throw them away!"

"Why?"

"The guy before you has done things that even I did not think were possible."

Fantastic.

I dress up with: white socks and white shoes, khaki colour Bermuda shorts with black leather belt and Hawaiian shirt. I'm the new Indiana Jones; just missing the whip.

Exiting my coffin worried like a lamb before the

Angry Waiters   *Federico Fumagalli*

slaughter, I meet Tomasz and his wife, the couple I saw on the airplane and at the Comfort Inn. He can speak Italian, for my own good, and he explains to me a little bit about this job. As I thought, there is *no* good news.

We take the lift and we climb up to the Horizon Court on Deck 14. The Horizon Court is a massive buffet open 24/7 that takes up all the length and width of this deck, decorated with blue fitted carpet, tables, armchairs, and open seats on the stern – the ass of the ship. In the middle there are swimming pools, bars, ice cream bars, pizzeria, and links with upper and lower decks.

My duty is to take away dirty plates from the tables, which is already a privilege for my first cruise as a Junior Waiter.

From now on something terrific sneaks inside me: the nightmare of USPH – United States Public Health, I suppose – that has an importance and power high enough to destroy the good things I learned about HACCP (Hazard Analysis and Critical Control Points). A mystery check by USPH in Italy would shut down many, many places in the hospitality industry.

On the DOTQCIG hygiene comes first, though I will soon find out that here *everything* comes first, for example hunger and tiredness.

Americans seem to have a particular hate for microbes: I don't think Americans cure illnesses; they ferociously kill every bacteria with any method, including a hammer.

~25~

Angry Waiters   *Federico Fumagalli*

The DOTQCIG has been 'Ship of the Month' for three consecutive months, claiming from ninety-five to ninety-nine per cent USPH score, but now that I am on board they can easily forget about reaching all those scores in the near future. I don't know yet how that works, but I bet that over here microbes are not allowed on board even with a passport. This ship has beaten the 'Queen Elizabeth' – another prestigious cruise ship – which not long ago has been plagued with an invasion of royal cockroaches.

Instead, we 'DOTQCIG Members', receive a real brainwashing about hygiene; it's a good idea, but there are so many rules and restrictions which are hard to go along with.

Suddenly somebody slams a blue towel (cleaning cloth) and a pair of disposable gloves in my hands: that's my equipment. With the towel I have to clean tables when Passengers leave. The towel has to be dipped in a solution of water and Chlorine, a kind of white powder that I have never heard of before, which would make the happiness of all the housewives who want to clean the house with a wide smile on their face.

Why do I need gloves? First of all, to avoid losing my fingerprints because of the chlorine; then because I am not allowed to touch anything with my own hands, in order not to contaminate absolutely anything and anybody. *Always* wear gloves. I have a couple of doubts: what if I need to tie up my shoe laces? Should I take my gloves off? No, I should do it hiding

Angry Waiters   *Federico Fumagalli*

somewhere, or change gloves right after. I could put them in chlorine for a few seconds and get them disinfected, but...

No! I may have the leprosy virus on my shoe laces and I could exterminate all Passengers.

On this ship there is no such a thing like clients or customers: there are only Passengers. Passengers are so important that they also have to be *pronounced* with a capital letter.

14.00: first Induction. What's that? It's a compulsory course regarding hygiene and safety on board and there are quite a few of them.

Together with Tomasz I come back to my cavern 3329 to take my Blue Card and my Life Jacket, which is bright orange. I close the door and get out, but the coming tragedy is on the way: there are two exits with one corridor, and...

No more Tomasz.

I don't want to call his name loudly, otherwise people may think that I am an idiot who lost his way -which is agonizingly true- but I can't find him. I go back and forth for the damn corridor, up the stairs and down again, I am lost and don't know where to go, but suddenly I feel something grabbing my arm: it's him, he drags me up to the Crew Bar were we sit among the other people waiting for the Captain to show up. In the silent waiting my stomach rumbles so much that I feel like everyone's heard it. On the other hand... when is lunch time? I'm hungry!

Angry Waiters   *Federico Fumagalli*

Eventually the Captain comes on stage: he passes word to somebody, who passes it to somebody else, and after the first few welcoming bullshits and jokes – which I don't understand, because my English sucks at jokes – we are asked how many of us are on their first cruise: I raise my hands shyly because I'm the only one among forty members. Everyone else has been here already once or twice, and probably they also know the trick of lunchtime. My stomach is the only one rumbling every two minutes.

All inductions are in English, nobody comes to translate them for me, so I have to pay very good attention because though I can (basically) speak and listen and read and write, many terms are unknown to me. I only hope nobody has the bad idea of asking me questions that require more than 'yes' or 'no'.

It's my lucky day: there is a video. We learn about four kinds of Fire Extinguishers, the correct use of the firebreak doors, the alarm systems location and emergency numbers to call, all things that I instantly forget.

It's now time to learn how to wear a Life Jacket and to memorize the respective alarm signal: seven short and one long blast. As soon as we hear them, no matter what we are doing – working, eating or *mating* – no matter where we are in the ship, we must stop whatever is going on and run to our cabin to pick up the Blue Card, the Life Jacket and a hat. I don't have one yet, and that's the reason why on the second Induction I am

Angry Waiters   *Federico Fumagalli*

told off by the man in charge, an Austrian F&B (Food and Beverage) Manager, tall and bald. After I picked everything up I should run like the wind to my Muster Station on Deck 5 as I am the A.P.P. (Assistant Passenger Party). This has nothing to do with celebrating Fire Spreading: my job is to calm down people even if we are sinking, saying that everything will be OK if they do what we say, helping them to wear Life Jackets though they are very well overweight and they could barely stay afloat, and then direct them toward the Lifeboats that scream 'NOOOOoooo!' as soon as they realise how massive these Passengers are.

Life safety on board is granted by the Crew, so it's a *must* that we know exactly what to do. For this specific matter there was once a thunderous laughter by the crew slagging off the instructor.

There was a funny joke by a colleague at dinner time in one of the dining rooms: during an exercise drill we heard the alarm, seven short and one long blast; all Passengers began flapping and he told them: "Don't worry! That iceberg is too far away!"

He was demoted.

At the moment of showing us the correct use of firebreak doors I show off my few intuitive abilities: the instructor says that these doors are located only on the 3rd, 4th and 5th floors. Their job is also to avoid water flooding in case we start sinking. The question is "Why are they located only on those low level floors?"

Nobody answers, so I shyly take my chance:

"Because after the 5th floor it's too late for everyone?"

Surprise: it's the correct answer. If the water has already flooded five floors, the chances that the ship will stay afloat long enough for us to survive are slim.

What do I win? I win the privilege of opening the firebreak doors pressing the appropriate button. Since I have this bad feeling that I will soon die sinking, I better know how to use them.

After the Induction I go back to my room losing my way again to put down my Life Jacket and the Blue Card, change uniform and run back on duty – late, because I get lost again – reaching the Bernini Dining Room. I hardly find it, but I find it. It would take me four days to learn that everywhere I need to go I first have to pass through the Crew Mess, the place where we are supposed to eat.

The problem is that first of all I need to learn how to reach the Crew Mess.

In the meanwhile, my lunch has gone to hell.

~~4~~
LOST IN BRATA

On board we don't get in the *shit:* there is a technical term we use instead: *brata*.

Brataiolo is anyone who gets in brata, which means getting so busy that you can call it shit.

Only later I will understand that we need to use the word *brata* because the management doesn't want to hurt the Passenger's sensitive feelings.

Sometimes I'm so much into it that I don't have time to send other people to hell, especially the ones who don't help: but here is the thing, nobody helps anybody. There's just no time for help, and when there is, what is missing is the will to do it. I only allow myself to swear at somebody if they try to play dirty with me; in that case, time lost is worth it.

I shout 'fuck off' to many Head Waiters sometimes, especially when they give me the infamous *'Caramella'*. Caramella in Italian means candy, but here it has another meaning: Caramella is the 'Last Minute Table', the last table available for running-late-people just one minute before closing the doors of the Dining Rooms. I have a bad feeling about this; indeed I get so many Caramellas that I could gain that one extra kilogram that the doctor advised I needed.

Moreover, when my colleagues find out that I live in a small town called Cremella (near Lake Como) the slagging goes on in every language spoken on board:

'The guy from Cremella takes the Caramella', spreads out quickly, and I begin to get pissed off more and more.

'Cippettone' is how we call a very stingy Passenger (Cippettone comes from Cheap, and though in Italian we don't have such a word, Cippettone can be the translation of Very Cheap, so Very Stingy). It's used when Passengers don't want to drink alcohol to avoid paying extras, but mostly to indicate one who *doesn't leave tips*.

'Rumenta' is somebody that sometimes places a complaint – Passenger or colleague – who is really, Really, REALLY a big asshole.

'Ronzata' (of which I am a greedy collector) is the telling off for when we make mistakes.

Brata, Caramella, Cippettone, Complaint, Ronzata and Rumenta: the perfect terminology for a great career.

First night, I'm in crazy ~~shit~~ brata because despite my late entrance in Bernini Dining Room – I got lost again– I know nothing about this dining room, this kind of service, rules, organisation, locations.

The first two very basic things that my Waiter Vincenzo yells at me are: 'YOU MUST FLY!' and 'LEARN TO STEAL!' and he is damn right. Also, I must be careful that nobody comes to steal my things in our station. What? Stealing? Why? Because we don't have enough stuff to carry on a decent service.

Starting from right now, until the end of my contract,

Angry Waiters   *Federico Fumagalli*

I will acquire a theft ability that I thought unthinkable. My wine opener will reveal to be a perfect tool to open locks.

Here is how ideologically a good shift is organised, with order and cooperation:

– At 16.30, I come on duty flying like a crow, I open my station and I start throwing glasses on the table before somebody comes to steal them. Then, given that surely there are not enough of them, I should go to steal more from the station of the ones who have not come in yet, or maybe I can take a look in the restaurant above where I can also take away some yellow and beige napkins. When I come back I finish the Mise en Place (French for 'set-up') with my Waiter and we lock the drawers for cutlery and chinaware with a solid padlock. Right after I fold yellow napkins for breadbaskets, ice buckets and service plates.

I fill three water jugs with water and ice using a scoop (using hands is not hygienic, and using glasses as scoops may break them), I put menus into their folders, I fill a small black box with ice, water and soap into which I will later on put dirty cutlery: on a cruise ship, in each station there's a big black box which contains a small black box. In the big one I put all the other dirty things: plates, side plates, saucers, cups.

On each BBB (Big Black Box) there is a number which should match with the number of the station.

Everyone must wash their own box, meaning that we have to bring it to the Indian dishwashers and come

~33~

Angry Waiters   *Federico Fumagalli*

back remembering the respective number. Glasses are washed in another machine that we personally have to attend.

Then I fill the creamers with milk and cream for coffee, I fill coffee pots with regular and decaf coffee, I walk around the kitchen to see where the food comes out and what kind, like starters, main courses, fish, meat, pasta, desserts… all in different and far-away-between-them places.

17.15: Meeting with Head Waiters that lasts around ten minutes, after which I have just a few minutes to scream and crash with the others to prepare butter, cheese containers, lemons, sauces and filling breadbaskets.

How do we fill a breadbasket? By covering our hands with a pair of latex gloves which, by never being in the appropriate gloves containers, must be stolen from somebody else, sometimes even reversing them inside out. Touch bread with your hands and you get in trouble: Passenger's extermination is behind the corner – I might have the Malaria virus hiding under my nails; also there is always a Head Waiter in patrol to check that everything is done in an Excellent way, where Excellent is the Brand Standard for everything, otherwise we are given a *Warning:* depending on the gravity of the Warning, or the number of them collected, I can easily be disembarked and left alone to my sad and useless destiny.

Once that I have conquered a glove or two, I'll keep

~34~

Angry Waiters   *Federico Fumagalli*

them for as long as possible.

One of the biggest nuisances of the service is that every single time I enter or exit the Galley I must change my tray. Service is done by carrying everything on big trays, stacking up to six plates on each pile, meaning that on each tray I should carry twelve plates covered with plastic transparent cloches (covers) to ensure that the food remains burning hot until is served. Even plates are burning, so much that from the kitchen counters I must take them with a napkin – that I don't always have time to take out of my pockets – or more often with my own hands at the speed of light in order to avoid losing my fingerprints. Each time I enter the galley with a tray it must be because I have something to give to the Indian dishwashers, but I have to put the tray down and pick up another clean one, even if mine isn't dirty. Each tray is washed at every passage. Sometimes I need to wait for a clean tray to appear from the washing machine, losing loads of time that usually I don't have. On the clean tray I will then put everything I need, trying to fill it up as much as possible to avoid useless extra trips back and forth. I have the doubt that carrying the same tray for five or six times without giving it to the dishwashers I could exterminate my entire station of six tables, about twenty people. At first I have the doubt; after some time I hope for it.

17.30: Doors of Heaven are opened to the Passengers: how can they be in a queue this early in the afternoon for dinner? When I was in kindergarten, 17.30 was 'Fruttolo' time! (Fruttolo is a kind of children's fruit flavoured yoghurt). I am not used to this, as wherever I've worked before, dinner starts around 7pm.

Americans always eat at any available moment, and my eyes witness that truly this is the population with the highest number of whale's butts, as I could see on TV. Some butts really spread out of chair's arms.

To pass into the galley from the dining room there are two revolving doors located on each side. Each door is divided by three internal compartments, turning ever after: it's not possible to stop them from rotating, first of all because we are supposed to walk in with a tray held with both hands; second because we don't have time to stop them; third because if we needed to stop them, it must be because there is an emergency: the only emergency is when we are trapped inside one of those compartments, and the button to stop them is outside. This means that someone else must be available to press the damn button, but as I said before, don't expect help from anybody.

Also, if we press the button, it might happen that the doors stop moving – when we are lucky-, or they start twisting like a blender – the other times.

You are not allowed to stop inside the compartment's doors, the reason being that you can't just stop them with your physical strength: they keep rotating like a blender and if you try to block them, they ground you

Angry Waiters   *Federico Fumagalli*

like coffee beans.

During service I must run – when it's quiet: I would say that I have to glide like a very pissed off dragonfly without touching the ground. If I run, I'm slow; if I run quickly, they overtake me; so I have to go… quicker! I must be hyper fast in everything because people have to eat and get the hell out of here to make space for other hungrier Passengers.

When people get up I must further heighten my pace: I have to clean dirty tables, wash my stuff, set tables again. Seems easy to say, but: in the Big Black Box there are three compartments, one for dessert plates, one for side plates and saucers, and one with the Small Black Box containing water, ice, soap, cutlery. Since my items are counted I have to quickly bring the whole BBB to the dishwashers; when I come out I have to carry a new tray and only then I can come back inside the galley with my dirty glasses in a secondary washing machine.

I must be aware of colleagues who might try to steal my glasses, while I try at the same time to steal some from them; it doesn't matter which glasses: water or wine glasses, it's just to have some extra in case of emergency or, more likely: *breakage,* of which I'm a proud expert. Theft strategies will sharpen up on daily basis; damage strategies, however, will not.

I bring back my glasses to the station, I run back in the galley to survey my BBB and, once ready, I have to polish cutlery dividing them by type on another tray and bring them back to the station balancing the tray on top of the BBB, and then I complete the tables set-up. When I think it's all done, my waiter reminds me that with new Passengers I have to refill butter with crushed ice on top, cheese containers, eventual sauces – sour cream, horseradish, cranberries sauce, mint sauce, BBQ... – and of course breadbaskets. But before I do that, I need to find a bloody latex glove, and once I find one I jealously keep it in my pocket, looking around to ensure that no Head Waiters have seen me. 'NO gloves in the pockets!' is another rule I'm happy to break.

Near the end of the service I start to feel hunger and thirst: obvious symptoms caused by my missed lunch and because whilst on duty it is absolutely forbidden to eat, munch or drink, even if it's a glass of water. I have to hide for it, but when I see all those security cameras I prefer not to do it. It's just for the bullshit stories of contamination of the USPH, that since the first day it really beats heavily on my balls. And I carry on my duty with symptoms that make me nervous over and over. Will it be like this every day? When can I get some food?

At 22.30 miraculously the shift is over and I can manage to drop down in Crew Mess to refuel at the Italian's table.

The Crew Mess is subdivided in Countries: the reason is that after one slaughtering day of English Speaking ('Only English must be spoken on duty!'),

Angry Waiters   *Federico Fumagalli*

everyone needs to swear and scream and complain in their own language. So: only Italian here; only Polish there; only Rumanian behind the corner; only Thai beside the TV; only Filipino near the drink machines; only Gay over there.

After that, I go back to my cabin, 3329 – Deck 3 India Section – where Robert M, my Polish roommate, explains to me how the cabin's cleaning works: first of all I need to *buy* my *Filipino* who makes my bed every day, brings to the laundry my dirty and sweaty underwear, cleans the floor – or at least he gives it a go – and puts my shoes and slippers away (I always keep them beside my bed, and every single night I have to search them in a different place; not that the place is big, but...). My uniform is washed for free, but my personal clothes need a payment, so when Mr Arlan (my Filipino) comes with clean items, he also brings the bill. The price for my new housewife is ten dollars per week, plus laundry and the compulsory tips it makes a total of fifteen to twenty dollars. I'm broke.

I could save money by washing my laundry myself, but time to go to the washing machines is missing. Even inside my cabin, washing something is impossible: my sink is as big as a cappuccino cup, inside which I can't wash more than a pair of underpants and a sock – not a *pair* of socks, just *one*. Besides, the water decreases because the plug for the sink doesn't exist at all, reason why I must block the hole with a latex glove, which very often is the same one I used during the day to pick up bread for my lovely Passengers. If I make too many bubbles the space for my underwear extinguishes, and time for self-laundry becomes ten times longer, considering that I have to separate white clothes from black and coloured, and bleach on board is forbidden (we have plenty of healthy Chlorine).

After some general and personal explanations and a little chat, I can finally set my alarm, remembering that on Saturdays I have to put the clock one hour forward →.

I sneak under my new clean bed sheets recalling every passage of my first day on a cruise ship, I think back to the day before when I took the airplane, I remember the Driver for the Comfort Inn, I think about the job, at how the Caribbean Islands might be in the next months; I wish not to meet this situation every day; eventually I fall asleep.

Exhausted.

Angry Waiters   *Federico Fumagalli*

~~5~~
DAY 2

My G-Shock alarm assaults me like a hunting lion and I am angry like a monkey because not only I slept badly, but also not enough.

I get up and ready for the second Induction located in a room that obviously I don't remember where it should be. I pick up my Blue Card and Life Jacket, I go out of the door silently avoiding waking up my room-mate and I try to figure out the way to the Crew Mess. The first thing I should learn is that wherever I need to go, I must pass through the Crew Mess.

Good. Got it.

What I didn't get yet is *how to get* to the Crew Mess. It's a labyrinth down here. But today seems to be my lucky day: on the way to nowhere I meet Stacy, a very smiley Mexican girl who is going to the Induction too. I join her and once in the right place I sit next to her. She might be useful for indications and many other interesting things.

As soon as the room fills up with people I notice that everybody is looking at me as if I were mentally retarded, laughing at my face without any consideration or respect. It takes me a while to realise that I am the only idiot who is actually *wearing* the orange life jacket: no one else has even bothered to bring it along, let alone wear it.

While I receive a fearsome bullying, I pray that the

Angry Waiters   *Federico Fumagalli*

ship would sink immediately and the firebreak doors at the 3rd, 4th and 5th floor wouldn't work.

Today the lesson is about causes and consequences of a contamination – which is unlikely to take place: virus fear getting on board. The USPH is acclaimed as the only remedy to save the world.

After a good portion of slides we watch a video: obviously it's an American-crap-style, like those movies where the superheroes defeat the bad guys, only that I witness scenes of virus and bacteria who launch a contamination attack to the ship and seize all Passenger's bodies where they will multiply spreading death all around. But:

just when I'm starting to be a supporter of the Streptococcus Tribe, the Ghostbuster's soundtrack explodes from the speaker, and members of the USPH burst on board armed with Chlorine ready to launch an antibacterial defence.

I'm having nausea; do they really want to inculcate us this bullshit?

The basic rule is to wash our hands. Absolutely right. Agreed. Clean thumbs up.

But didn't they tell us that we are not allowed to touch anything?! There are loads of mini-sinks spread out everywhere, ready to receive our unlikely greasy hands. There's the need of washing hands after bringing a tray to the Indians; after touching food – which we should never touch; after coughing and sneezing; touching hair, face, nose, ears, mouth, brain;

Angry Waiters   *Federico Fumagalli*

after eating or drinking – both absolutely forbidden; picking something up from the floor; tying up shoelaces; putting hands in our pockets; every twenty minutes even in case we had not touched anything, because virus jump and float in the air. So, where the hell should I put my hands? I have an idea, but then I would have to wash them again.

For a poor virus there is no way to put a family together. In our station there is a divisor glass for 'Clean Area' and 'Dirty Area'. Our glasses are not washed, but sterilised in a glass machine at two thousand degrees Fahrenheit; don't know how they don't break into pieces.

End of this Induction, we have a brief introduction towards the next one where we will be explained the correct use of four different Fire Extinguishers: 'Powder', 'Water', 'Foam', 'CO_2', each one aimed for a different purpose and type of fire. We must be able to use the correct fire extinguisher for the proper fire, and also recognise what kind of fire extinguisher Must Not Be Used with the wrong fire: for example, never use a Water fire extinguisher against fire caused by electrical failure. It gets you a serious electrical shock as water is a perfect electrical conductor. Since I have this feeling that I will soon die blazing, I better learn all about them.

Then I just have time to change uniform and dress up in Horizon Court style with my flowery green shirt, beige Bermuda short pants and white socks and shoes;

Angry Waiters   *Federico Fumagalli*

time is just enough for me to swallow two half mouthfuls of lookalike food and start working from 11.30 to 16.00.

At exactly 16.03 I rush in my cabin again for shower and another uniform change: tonight I need the black vest for Gala, then I rocket myself to Bernini Dining Room at 16.30. Really, it seems I've got no time for myself! Is it like this every day?!

No, indeed: it's going to be worse.

During my rocketing run toward the dining room I lose my orientation, but luckily I meet Sakorn who helps me find the way.

I enter Bernini and exactly as the day before I better be prepared to get in deep brata with my waiter, who starts whipping me with so much information that my atomic brain smoothly manages to forget. Otherwise I couldn't quite explain why a couple of Passengers accused me of not singing 'Happy Birthday to You' at their birthday, as it should happen whenever there is a birthday on board so all Passengers are happy and we lose loads of time, because to sing Happy Birthday we must gather in a group of at least six waiters, leaving three stations temporarily without service and with the guard down: when the singing waiters go back to their station, surely something has mysteriously disappeared (Water glasses? Coffee cups? Water jugs? You name it), and also we have to listen to other Passenger's moaning because their food is late. Come on! You are not starving! You've got such a big reserve of fat!

But at the end of the night, when I haven't yet learned the Dirty Way to have dinner – indeed I skipped dinner – I walk down in the Crew Mess watching the other people eating and then go straight to my coffin, dead. Even for eating I need to practise my theft strategies, given that if I want to avoid the shit of the Crew Mess's Chef, I need to steal from the kitchen.

~~6~~
BASIC SHI(F)TS

The shifts I'm usually on duty for as a Junior ~~Slave~~ Waiter are:
1: Lido Breakfast
2: Lido Lunch
3: Dining Room

The names of the Dining Rooms are:
– Bernini
– Donatello
– Canaletto

And then there are millions of other micro-duties in which I stumble without mercy: Teatime, Wine Tasting, Napkin Folding, Champagne Waterfall, Island Night, Embarkation, Canapés and more and more to add to the basic three.

Also, I must include in the list all the pain-in-the-arse wasting time duties; each one of us has the same thought about them: In Port Manning, Inductions, Bow Drills, Crew Rounds, Galley Round, Time Windows (which are thirty minute periods of time when *nobody* is allowed to enter or exit the ship), eventual extra meetings – as if two each day weren't enough.

And then there are the Side Jobs, extra jobs that some of us truly ask to be assigned on besides the normal duty. The reason is that some of these Side Jobs allow the person who performs them to always have Saturday morning off in Fort Lauderdale. As long as they are happy, I let them do the Side Jobs.

It had happened to me that I began my service in Bernini dining room for two reasons: first because I could have an Italian waiter to explain me things in a quicker way, given that speed is everything and my English is nothing; second, Bernini is the easiest of the dining rooms, where service is 'quiet'.

What?! Indeed I will later find out that the other two dining rooms are real cruel battlefields.

But in Bernini I start earlier. Why? Because as I said, at 17.30 Americans are already following the kilometric queue to dine, so that later they can also go cramming with free food on the buffet to the Horizon Court, open 24/7.

I can see they have nothing to do – on the other hand they are on holiday – and since they can't walk the dog, the cat or the crocodile, at least they bring their stomach to experience something new.

Right after the meeting, we Junior Waiters and Buffet Stewards rush into the galley 'quietly and tidily' like a herd of bison charging toward the 'Frutteria' (Fruit Station) where we try to get hold of 'Butter-lemon-cheese' with six butter containers with crushed ice on top, a bowl with lemon wedges and cheese container with grated cheese, even though I never understood if the guys behind the counter use the appropriate grater

Angry Waiters   *Federico Fumagalli*

or if they grate parmesan cheese with their teeth.

While waiters stand at the doors to welcome the Passengers, we fill the creamers with milk and cream and then we worry about coffee pots with both types of coffee. Those two things, up to a little while ago, were allowed to be done before the meeting; now we have to wait until the last moment, in service time, losing loads of time that we don't usually have. Entering the galley only to fill two creamers? No way!

Getting back to the station I switch on the internal heater for cups and coffee pots, because they need to be warmed up. Saying 'warming up' isn't right: better say 'scorching up'. After ten minutes you *don't want* to touch them, don't even think about it. You need a yellow napkin folded in at least four layers, or you lose your fingers.

Later we can start various war scenarios against Passengers and of course against work*mates* too. Here there are no friends, favours don't occur, and only the smartest survive.

News of the day: paper doilies for butter, side plates, starter plates, butter forks. Are they going to give us more stuff? Of course not, but they expect us to improve the service even if we are short of items, using our very limited number of available things like cutlery or plates or glasses. And the worst is that the Head Waiters don't care about us losing time on duty to put doilies everywhere, these little round papers stick together and there is no way to separate them unless we have a sharp nail or we lick our fingers in front of Passengers. It's not the Head Waiters who have to run.

Bernini is absolutely the same as Donatello Dining Room which stands one floor above. For shape and disposition of tables, I wouldn't recognise them without going out to look at the bright sign, or if I don't enter the galley. The other dining room, Canaletto, is a little different, but the style is the same. Canaletto is also called Traditional Dining Room.

In Bernini there's the Pantry where we keep the pre-ordered wines during the Wine Tasting: every Monday afternoon some of the Waiters have to be in duty from 15.00 to 16.30; they find the dining room already set-up, because in the morning we Junior Waiters in Dining Room shift, *after* cleanings but *before* breakfast must load trays of glasses from Donatello dining room and bring them down here. After that, we set them on the tables following some paper layouts: for each person who does the tasting there should be four wine glasses, one water glass and one flute for champagne.

Once Wine Tasting is done, the striking charge of Junior Waiters is ready to attack the glass washer, each one of us ambushed around it and armed with a big tray, waiting to steal as many glasses as possible to return them to their own station. We waste up to fifteen minutes – absolutely outrageous – to refill a single tray, because most of the times it's forty of us trying to grab

Angry Waiters   *Federico Fumagalli*

one or two glasses each for every round of washing, and we need twenty glasses to refill one tray. When we have filled it up, after fighting with the ones who are trying to steal glasses from our own trays, and also after having had a few shouts with the Indian Dishwasher's Manager who doesn't want to see a herd of fools around his glass machine, and who wants us to pile up our trays one on top of the other *with* the glasses on them, then, only then, we can come back to our stations. What we leave behind us is an astonishing mess of debris and shattered glasses everywhere, but on the other hand is not possible to order us to line up in a queue and take a rack each. It would be possible if it weren't for Rumanian people, who have the inner spirit at the art of stealing, a little bit like Italians from Naples, who I consider the Masters of Theft.

Theft, once again, is a kind of skill that I'm learning quicker and quicker every day, because if I want to finish on time, I need to be smarter and beat them by playing their own game.

I bring glasses to my station and I hide them otherwise they steal them, I run up to Donatello to take white tablecloths and yellow napkins; when I come back I realise that my glasses are still all there, but all my three water jugs have disappeared. Bastards!

But no problem: against *bastarding* there is a remedy. I follow my pissed off instinct and move bloody fast and furtively to steal three water jugs not from one station only – it would be too obvious – but from three

~50~

Angry Waiters   *Federico Fumagalli*

of them, so that after my passage there will be not only one Junior Waiter, but three of them running around like fools to get them back, and while they are all away I can take advantage of the situation and have another go to their unguarded stations, with discretion, to get a teapot from one, two glasses from another one, three cups from the third.

I bring back my loot and start my mise en place. Once the tables are completed, usually nobody touches them, so I can stay relatively unworried. Then I go in the galley to fill my water jugs and everything else. In Bernini there are two Water Refilling Stations, each one inside the galley, next to the rotating doors, and it's very comfortable, not like in Donatello, where there is only one water station, and the ones who work in the right side of the dining room must run to the left side to fill the jugs. It's a long way.

The galley is also smaller, though it looks very big, because it's used to serve only Bernini, and sometimes in one line of counters (called pass), chefs serve two different dishes instead of only one. In Donatello, instead, the galley is double the size because it serves two dining rooms: it's like having the galley in the middle, with Donatello on one side and Canaletto on the other. That means double waiters and double mess. When I finish my business I set foot in the station, sit down for the ten minutes briefing, and then wait for the usual agony of service. Thing number one to annoy me is: the music played. Chill-out music, popular folk with

Angry Waiters   Federico Fumagalli

accordion, slow trumpets, very sad melodies, which the management think to be suitable for Passengers, but absolutely unbearable for a heavy metal-head like me. Besides, I get many bad comments from Passengers too, especially when CDs are played at random; there are these three or four songs that jam and we need to send somebody to press the button 'forward →'.

When Passengers come in, I pull the chair backward, I seat them, and as soon as they put their butts down I try to push the chair in its previous position. Unfortunately, this is not that easy: as I said, the Americans on average are well overweight. I can't always push the chair forward. Some asses are so prominent that if feel lucky not to be born a *chair*.

In addition to that, even without Passengers, wooden chairs are a nightmare to drag around on the carpeting because they don't slip, so I'm forced to move them gently with a kick.

When Passengers have taken their seats I open the napkin on their lap, making the shape of a triangle; while the Waiter gives the menu, I serve iced tap water – purified tap water – from the jugs into their glasses trying not to drop anything, because ice cubes have this unfair habit of sticking in the tip of the jug, blocking the normal flow of water making it drop around and out and everywhere, except than inside the glass. Passengers think that I'm not capable of such a simple task like refilling a water-glass, and they doubt about my other abilities. How to blame them?

I grab the breadbaskets and go to refill them; if I am lucky, in my pocket I still have the same latex glove I used the day before to wash my smelly socks, otherwise I have to wonder why the glove containers are always empty and try to steal one.

In the galley there are three large baskets of different bread, including bread-sticks of which I'm greedy, and looking inside I ask myself: 'Why the hell don't we use tongs?' Answer: Because we don't have any. And if we had them, they would be lost or stolen.

I come back in the dining room with the breadbaskets and I put them on the tables hoping that the bread would not get devoured straight away otherwise I have to run another trip in the galley. The thing is that I can't take extra bread for stock to my station. Only "When you get the fucking Passengers, you can get the fucking bread! Understand?!", the Head Waiters told us.

After all this, my Italian Waiter introduces himself and his assistant (me). Sometimes he welcomes Passengers at the tables by performing a terrible version of "'O sole mio", which I find embarrassing not only because I wholeheartedly hate that song, but also because Passengers expect me to sing it along with him. I would rather put a tarantula in my underwear.

Finally, I start taking the drinks order, trying to push for alcoholic drinks (Push for the wine!) rather than Ice tea: in this case I have to bear the pain of running around looking for highball glasses that I can never find anywhere, refilling them with three ice cubes (no more, no less: *must be* three), one slice of lemon, one straw and then I press the button on the machine for tea. Non-alcoholic drinks are free, but alcoholic drinks are another story: we charge for them, and indeed we are supposed to get a percentage on those drinks we sell, but it goes without saying that I have never seen an extra dollar. I take the order, I go get them, I serve them, and my Waiter takes the money: nice and simple.

My Waiter takes the food order, and from now on I can start to run like a cheetah throwing the service tray on the station and launching plates on the tables as if they were Frisbee. This kind of fast service is called 'Butta Giù' (from the Italian *buttare* – to throw away – and *giù* – down; giving something in a rush to somebody without showing a little bit of respect, like 'Throw it down and get lost!').

At 22.00 doors are closed and I invoke the Gods of Tiredness for not giving me a Caramella, one Last Minute Table, otherwise I finish too late and the food I learnt to steal gets cold, not to say anything about my precious six flavours of ice cream whose scoops are melting away in one undistinguishable piece of mud.

Another thing they use to do in Bernini is the 'Shopping Mall', where somebody sells signed products with the "Daughter of the Queen" logo and various gadgets to increase the revenue. For this, I need to start earlier on looking for chairs with the same colour that for the occasion have been spread everywhere. What's more, I need to clean my station's floor of all the small pieces of rubbish paper using a brush that is never in the same place; and do you know how hard it is to pass a brush on a carpet? Rubbish hops left and right and back and forth, but never inside the scoop.

Just for the pleasure of wasting time.

~~7~~
DONATELLO DINING ROOM

The main difference between Donatello and Bernini is the double-sized kitchen. Donatello is more used: we make breakfasts, lunches, dinners, Teatimes, meetings, Bow Drills, and sex (Yes: sex!): today a condom has been found behind a station and it has clearly been used. Judging by the colour it's easy to guess *how*. The Headwaiter who made this discovery tells us: "Whoever it was, they have been very clever to use a condom. Not so much to leave it here. Now someone has to clean this. I'm gonna choose randomly the lucky one."

General moaning of us all Junior Waiters.

"OK" He points at me. "You, the guy from Cremella…"

Everyone laughs.

"Eh no, I already take the Caramella!" I complain.

"Come on, today you, tomorrow someone else." He commands.

'*Bring me your sister tomorrow, I'll show her how to use a condom*' I think to myself, ☺ing at him and going to pick up some cleaning items and the glove that I will later use to pick up the bread.

I should arrive on duty at 16.45, something that never happens. I always arrive at 16.30 otherwise I wouldn't find any more glasses. Meeting time is set for 17.45

Angry Waiters   *Federico Fumagalli*

and doors open at 18.00.

When I arrive I find the people who are still doing the Teatime and a very big dirty mess; if Passengers are gone I can start my mise en place, steal glasses from someone who have stolen from me previously, search for some open stations from which to borrow something that I swear to God I will never return, like saucers, side plates, cups, breadbaskets, and why not: the cheese container. I do whatever I have left to do and after the drowsy meeting I run to the galley to overtake the queue for 'lemon-butter-cheese', because in addition to Donatello's colleagues there are also Canaletto's.

Now I should respect the very new rule about bread: as I said before, 'Only when you get the fucking Passengers, you can get the fucking bread! Understand?!' and those are Headwaiter's words. But rules are meant to be broken, and seeing that somebody is already playing dirty, I decide to play dirty too: I fill my tray with all my six breadbaskets and come back to my station quick like a greyhound, but my luck remains stuck on the leash because on the way out I find a Headwaiter who catches me guilty with stolen goods in my hands, and zero Passengers in my tables. I get an unbelievable *'Ronzata'* – I get shit from this prick – and I go on thinking that is much better if I leave this place. I'm tired of being told off for bullshit like this, but with a little bit more patience we will all arrive in Europe, where everything will be easier.

Angry Waiters   *Federico Fumagalli*

Here too, as in Bernini, service goes on wonderfully, and I'm as happy as a grumpy Polar Bear in a cage. I ride like a horse, sweat like a pig, dehydrate like a stranded jellyfish, wait for closing doors time hoping not to take a Caramella – I already took a used condom – I try to get rid of the last dining people, wash my box, take my ice cream and together with my now-cold stolen main course I lock my station and disappear to the Crew Mess.

One of the ugly things of Donatello is that the kitchen, being in the middle of two dining rooms, gives me trouble: sometimes, often, every time, I need to reach a Pass to get a main course and what do I find ahead of me? A queue of fifteen people. My heart stops beating. It can't be true! Passengers outside are hungrily waiting for me to reappear ASAP! They are sharpening knives and forks! I can hear them yelling!

But to sooth the pain there's the rule which says that whoever has to take *only one* plate can overtake everybody else, shouting 'One Main à-la-mano!' ('One main straight away! On my hand!')

But it's sad – and nobody in the ship likes it – to make all these battles with eyes that just want to shut from tiredness; arms that get sore if you are not used to heavy weights; we have to carry trays with up to fourteen plates on them – the limit is twelve, but why should I do another trip? – risking to drop them because they wobble along, the ship sways, and because I can't see ahead looking between the two

Angry Waiters   *Federico Fumagalli*

plate towers: in between them I have to place bottles and drinks, so I have to travel with a radar hoping not to crash into something or somebody.

Somebody could get backache problems from the wrong way they carry the Big Black Box: being a cube you can easily place the heavy items on one side which you should rest against your belly, and not using your arms completely stretched out. If the weight is positioned randomly, it will make you bend your back backward, and it's a mistake that will give pain with time. Make a little effort at the beginning and you will save your back, besides building up a little extra strength. My trick for when I am very exhausted is to put the bottom of the box on the top of my belt, which has a large metal lock. That gives me a little relief.

Plus, we have to become masters of balance: when the BBB is washed and cutlery is already polished and placed on the tray on top of the box, and if by coincidence the glasses are also ready and we can't take the risk of them getting stolen, we must organise the weight load: box underneath, tray on top with heavy cutlery in the middle toward our chest, glasses on the outside. And take care of sea waves and revolving doors, which are just a little bit larger than our trays.

Once I set everything back in the station, I keep on running, smiling to my Passengers as if I had a dental prosthesis.

~~8~~
CANALETTO DINING ROOM

Canaletto is the most hated, because here we work really hard and we finish later than anywhere else.

This is the 'Traditional Dining Room', where the Passengers are always the same all along the cruise if no trouble happens, but trouble is always behind the corner – and there are heaps of corners – beginning from the fact that there are two Sittings: the first is at 18.15 and we need to march by carefully keeping in mind that we have to get rid of our Passengers by 20.00; any later is too late.

We should begin duty at 16.45, but I always arrive at 16.30 otherwise I can't conclude anything, given that my Waiter (a different one) has this friendly habit of being late no matter what and of not helping me do anything. He comes and he disappears to talk with somebody; when he reappears he looks sweaty as if he had pushed the ship himself. Since he looks so tired, he kindly asks me if I can also do this and that, quicken up my pace, help him to avoid mistakes and bla bla bla. I mutter that I would kindly smash a tray onto his baldy forehead, but I don't do it because I don't have time to clean up afterwards.

Before setting foot in Canaletto, I have to drop in to Donatello to pick up tablecloths and yellow napkins.

I catapult myself in Canaletto and, if I'm lucky, I find chairs and tables exactly as I left them the previous

Angry Waiters   *Federico Fumagalli*

day; if I'm unlucky – almost every time – I find only the tables, and between swearing and cursing I have to run around other tables of other stations to steal chairs with the same colour from the ones who have taken them from me, always using my system of stealing one chair on each station, in order to provoke disorder and chaos in as many stations as possible. Sometimes my colleagues are very upset with me because I act like a bastard, but here we all belong to the same family, we are all the same, and if I weren't a bastard, I wouldn't survive. I can't let anybody take over me, otherwise fifteen years of Karate and all the survival skills I learnt would be wasted. So... I carry on *bastarding* left and right.

Sometimes the bloody chairs are hidden in a hidey-hole behind the Security Exit Doors that in case of emergency would never open; this would lead to the certain death of all Passengers stuck in there, be it for asphyxia, be it burnt alive, be it for the headbutts that soon I will start to unleash.

I set the chairs by colour, I put down glasses – if I have them – I steal glasses – if I don't have them. But for fuck's sake! Two thousand eight hundred Passengers, three dining rooms, two hundred waiters, and I have to sweat to get a few items. They are not even enough for one decent service, and this should be a luxury cruise, one of the best in the world! WTF?!?

Depending on the day of the week I need to fold napkins in a different way: Saturdays, Tuesdays and

~61~

Angry Waiters   *Federico Fumagalli*

Fridays are 'flat'; Sundays and Thursdays are Gala Dinner, so I have to make 'fans'; on Mondays they become 'small boats'; on Wednesdays I make 'long hats'; on *Shit*days I can put *toilet paper*.

Meeting is at 17.30, and at the end of it a Headwaiter chooses four brave men who must distribute bread to everybody, using of course two pairs of latex gloves. Here we have the chance to place breadbaskets on the tables straight away because Passengers enter all at the same time. In Canaletto I take part in a parade of Junior Slaves holding trays full of empty breadbaskets that ask nothing but to be refilled.

While I wait for the chefs to come upstairs with the big boxes of bread from Bernini, I get hold of another tray for the usual trio lemon-butter-cheese, hoping that nobody has stolen my cheese container while I am going to put down the breadbasket's tray.

After a queue formed by Junior Slaves coming from both Donatello and Canaletto, I run back to the station to put butter containers on the side-plates with shrimp-forks and the doilies on the tables, lemon and cheese inside the drawer. In the meanwhile I notice something strange (but not so surprising): looking in the clean area I try to convince myself that what I see is not true; it can't be true, it must not be true, but unfortunately it is true and there's nothing I can do about it: somebody took two of my three water jugs already refilled. And now my Waiter comes to give me shit because the jugs are missing. You idiot! What are you supposed to do

Angry Waiters   *Federico Fumagalli*

in the station?! Comb your bald head? Buttering your dildos?

Trying to clarify the situation is useless, time is running out, it's 18.10 and in five minutes doors will be open to the herd for the First Sitting and I still have to get my brea...

My Bread!

Hell! I forgot!

I run damn quickly to the place where I left my tray, and with no surprise at all one breadbasket is missing. I have six tables and only five breadbaskets; I'm going to get a complaint either from the Passengers or from my Waiter or from some Supervisor, or all together.

Also, I'm the last one in the queue and I risk remaining breadless – bread rolls are counted out by the chefs; I don't know how, but I manage to refill all of them getting the very last bread roll. I dry my forehead with my sleeve, making sure that nobody has seen me otherwise I should go and wash my hands in one of those thousands of mini-sinks.

Running back to my station I'm blocked by the incoming Passengers who don't move away even under threat, so I need to make my way by smashing their ribs with my elbows, and in the general mess I take back two water jugs from somewhere. Then I start the same agony of service, but depending on the day there is something extra to do, as if the usual things weren't enough.

Besides moving my ass quicker than usual because at

~63~

Angry Waiters   *Federico Fumagalli*

20.30 'Starts the Second Sitting!' in Canaletto there can be a different dessert (banana split with cherry), or 'Penne all'Arrabbiata' – Italian pasta with red hot chilli pepper – all things that luckily are made by the Head Waiters in person on the trolleys, one of the rare occasions in which I can really see Head Waiters doing some work for real. I've always thought a *working Head Waiter* was just a mythological creature, never seen before, but no: they really work, once a week, for a couple of hours.

But the thing that all Passengers crave with greed is the 'Baked Alaska'.

~~9~~
THE BAKED ALASKA

The Baked Alaska is a mountain of spongy cake covered with soft meringue and filled with chocolate and vanilla ice cream. On top of each Baked Alaska there is a small candle, the sort of short candles you usually find at your local cemetery. We Junior Slaves form a long, long queue behind the entrance of the restaurant with our nice and heavy whole Baked Alaska on the shoulder, and a powerful voice comes out of the dining room's speakers telling us that we can all go and fuck ourselves.

No, obviously not: the speakers announce to the Passengers that *they* can go and fuck themselves.

No, no, no: I must be really exhausted. The speakers say to the Passengers that in *one second* they will be watching The Amazing Parade of The Junior Slaves and their Baked Alaskas. Just like in a circus, where we are the animals.

Party music sparks up suddenly. Somebody is in charge to lit up our candles, room's lights go down and we bravely enter the dining room like a train of fools, smiling and singing and walking and dancing and twerking around every table, while all Passengers sing and take pictures and scream and incite us to continue forever.

There is so much noise and everything is so loud that I take advantage of the situation to release some very

Angry Waiters   *Federico Fumagalli*

angry and powerful burps, trying hard to blow off the row of burning candles ahead of me. I feel a real idiot dancing with this Baked Alaska on my shoulder, so I burp out loud to declare my opposition to the world.

I doubt that anyone has heard me, but I'm sure that many Passengers have seen my ugly face in action.

End of the parade; I run back to my station, because the two-minutes-ago-happy-Passengers are now screaming and demanding their Baked Alaska as if this was the last thing they would do in life. Brandishing forks and spoons, they threaten me as if I'm neglecting their bellies. They are almost upset because I'm not giving them portions as big as the ones the waiter in the other station is giving to his Passengers.

OK, I got it: you don't want to give tips on this cruise; Cippettone and rumenta!

Usually in Canaletto we finish much later than in other dining rooms, and it's more difficult to steal food from the kitchen.

At the end of the night I feel knackered – if everything went well – my eyes are easily closing down, and after dinner which is always around midnight, I retire myself in my own coffin where I do my forty press-ups with clenched fists, shower and I fall asleep ready to start straight after. Sometimes, I'm so tired that I dream the phases of service; this is too much: I don't want to dream I'm still working!

~~10~~
LIDO BREAKFAST

05.15

What the hell! I don't have time to go to bed that I already have to wake up. It's 05.15 and my numb mind gets number from my G-Shock beep alarm.

I switch it off, moving my hand around trying hard to find the light switch that stands behind my sleepy head, but tiredness manages to overcome me, and I fall asleep again.

05.18

I suddenly wake up widening my eyes: earthquake! Massive vibrations! Ocean-quake! We are all going to die!... but then I realise it's just the time for my second alarm, the one that comes from my phone in vibration mode, so I am condemned to start another research of the light switch, at which click I get a disco-like rage projected at my foggy eyes.

With anger and despair I get up from my bloody bed cursing, showering, shaving my ugly face and wearing my Safari-man uniform: flowery green shirt, beige short pants and a pair of white socks and white shoes. The company, at the moment of giving me the contract, has been very clear: 'No marks or brands on socks and shoes! They must be white and white!'

I had to cut off the Nike logo on seven pairs of socks, only to come on board and notice that nobody cared of that rule. Somebody even had a yellow smiley face painted on their socks. One girl had 'left' and 'right' written on her socks, only to wear them the other way round. My broken socks look ridiculous, and I have to roll them down completely so that no one can see I cut them. I hate everybody.

I walk up to the Horizon Court, and at 05.45 I start working. 05.45 for one whole long week. It's not much comfort knowing that I will probably finish at 11.30 because, if the ship is at sail, the only clever thing that's left to do, after what somebody dares to call 'lunch', is put my head down.

After the early morning meeting we have a break for our breakfast and then we come back at 06.30.

But what's the meaning of that? Why can't we arrive at 06.20 for the meeting and start straight away after? For one week each one of us has to carry on the same duty; there is no reason to be briefed every day, we know the situation, it's always the same story: Smile ☺, Never Say No, Push for the Wine!, are the three basic rules, but they could save us at least the last one: we are doing breakfast!

At 06.30 we really start, and here is a list of various tasks under which we can perform our Slave's skills: …

COFFEE TROLLEY

For the sleepiest of us, because we can lean on the

Angry Waiters   *Federico Fumagalli*

trolley while pushing it back and forth along our side of buffet, asking the Passengers what they would like to drink: "Coffeeeeee? Teeeeea? Cream in the coffeeeee?"

It's quite boring, and the small coffee pots must be refilled after every ten coffees and by doing so we have to go back to the coffee refilling stations spread at the corners of the long buffet.

If children are around, we play *crash and burn* with those little pests who run and jump everywhere and come up like wild mushrooms from under the tables. We just can't see them.

If the crash happens at high speed (their speed, of course: our trolleys on the carpet don't travel fast) it's more dangerous because the scorching coffee pots unbalanced on top risk falling straight in their face. Of course, we might get a *Warning* because in their parents' minds, it's not *their kids* who are running like rats in the middle of our job, but it's *us* who have not successfully avoided them.

And who said that we *have to* avoid them?

SEGRETARIO

Segretario in Italian means 'Secretary', in Italy the typical guy who works as an office worker.

But not here.

Usually they choose somebody from the Philippines or Thailand for this job: Segretario is the one that at the beginning of Lido Breakfast prepares the 'Blue Towels, Chlorine and Gloves' in all the six boxes (stations) and during service walks around those boxes to collect rubbish bags, four for each station, brings them down to the incinerator on Deck 4 for burning, and changes bags.

As per today, the reason why it always has to be Philippines and Thailand still remains unknown.

JUICE

Service assigned to the ones with lack of willpower: just stay behind the counter serving grapefruit and orange juice from two big jugs. We might just move two metres if somebody asks for another kind of juice, or if we have to replace clean glasses. After four hours we eventually fall asleep in the grapefruit juice, or we have cramps.

CLEANING LINE

Unluckily, I don't have such a privilege. Cleaning Line Slave works inside the buffet, only half side of it; grabbing a blue towel and a little empty cereal bowl, they should go around the line of food brushing away breadcrumbs and small pieces of food that Passengers spread all along the wooden shelves. It seems like Passengers can't manage to use tongs or a spoon and fork used as clippers in one hand, like that lady who

Angry Waiters   *Federico Fumagalli*

tried to get a slice of bread holding the clippers with both hands, without managing the operation, gave up the slice of bread, walked around the buffet suspiciously, came back to the breadbaskets and took the slice with her hands. Unfortunately, the slice of bread slipped away from her hands, falling on the floor. So what? She leant down, grabbed it, and put it back in the breadbasket.

I watch her from outside, shaking my head, but I don't care: I leave the dirty and dusty slice in the basket, ready for the next Passenger to get it. In the same moment I am on duty as:

COLLECTING PLATES AND CUPS

With my big luck, and for the fact that I hardly feel physically tired (what really breaks me down is the Mental Stress), when I'm on duty Collecting Plates and Cups I never find a trolley available, therefore I must walk back and forth to my three stations collecting all the Brown boxes with dirty mugs, cups, saucers and whatsoever and bring them to wash. I bring back the clean Brown box in the station and I go to another one.

Same thing for the plates, which, on the other hand, wait for me under the shape of unbelievably heavy mountains, and to pass through the small doors leading to the Indian dishwashers I have to turn oblique and kick them (kick the doors, not the dishwashers).

Little note: I keep saying Indian Dishwashers. This

Angry Waiters   *Federico Fumagalli*

has nothing to do with racism or hate; first of all, I know the correct term is Kitchen Porters and not Dishwashers, but on board everyone calls them Dishwashers: who am I to call them properly?

Second: they are all Indian. All of them.

COLLECTING SILVER

Same story: I take the Brown Box and I go around the stations collecting cutlery for washing. I wash them, destroying my eardrums because of the noisy washing machine (cutlery is not a dishwasher's job; it's our job) and start again.

REPLACING PLATES

The opposite: I have to collect clean plates from the dishwashing area and put them on the buffet. Sometimes I come out with towers of plates as high as the Leaning Tower of Pisa and some very brainy Passenger stands ahead of me, blocking my passage. I unblock the idiot shouting "Andiamo!" (Come on! Move!). Or rather, even worse, somebody with a resigned brain, though seeing me with an ancient tower of heavy plates in my hands, dares to stop me and ask me where he can find the restrooms: "Ma ti ci mando io al restroom se non sposti il culo!" (I'll send you to the restroom myself if you don't move your ass!), obviously ☺ing sincerely. One time an old lady asked

Angry Waiters   *Federico Fumagalli*

me the time: how the hell am I supposed to look at my watch?! Burn, witch!

A bellicose American arrives and stops me while my plate tower is deciding either to fall left or right of me and he asks me: "Excuse me, can I have a cup of coffee Decaf?", to whom I answer, jokingly: "Sorry, no more Decaf! Try on the *Not So Tiny* Daughter of the Queen (*Not So Tiny* is the twin ship of the *Coloured With Gold*)!", but the monkey on holiday doesn't get the joke: "I don't really like your humor, my friend."

"I don't like you, my friend." and I leave him there with his own caffeine problem, caffeinically ignoring him.

REPLACING THE COFFEE STATION

Surprise! Everything is missing! The night workers didn't set anything. There is not one single item in place.

There you go, how annoying, I have had enough of it even before starting my shift, because now I must complete the job of the ones who left it half done.

Then, first of all, already pissed off at such an early hour in the morning, I have to look for cups from the Indian dishwashers, who of course haven't even switched on the machine, just because it's *me* on duty today. For some reason they don't like me. But I don't like them either, since I don't exactly greet them cheerfully every morning with a bunch of flowers.

Angry Waiters   *Federico Fumagalli*

I threaten them to call a Supervisor, and as by magic the washing machine roars up its powerful engine and the Indians multiply from two to four: one sprouts out from under the glasses' shelf, another one suddenly opens the cabinet door with eyes half closed. In two minutes I find myself embracing four racks of clean and disinfected cups, about ninety, just enough for thirty people, because the average usage is about three cups per cranium.

In the meanwhile I'm going to run out of lemons, and I run to replace lemon slices for Iced Teas.

No more ice in the bucket, so I refill it: after that I refill teabags (around ten types of tea), the creamers, paper cups (for these I need to ask for the storeroom's key to the Segretario, but every research is futile because he is obviously hidden somewhere smoking or eating in the Crew Mess). Last thing: plastic cups and two plates with clippers for lemon slices and the scoop for ice cubes.

OK, now that everything is set in order, I go to chat a little bit with somebody until the first Passengers come; besides, my side of buffet (today Starboard side) will open a little later.

Yet, something is wrong. I'm not quiet. I feel it. Something disturbs me, an alarm that signals me that I missed something. I feel this signal growing stronger and stronger; Oh, Yes, it's really one of my Head Waiters poking my shoulder to let me know that I forgot to refill *all* the sugar sets.

Angry Waiters   *Federico Fumagalli*

NOOO!

Running to the Buffet Locker I put as many sugar sachets as possible in a big, Big, BIG container: white sugar, brown sugar, green sugar, Sweet'n Low (pink), Sweetener (blue), *Sweatner* (bleah). What is the difference between the pink and the blue one? Nobody knows.

During service, if it's busy, the coffee stations under my control are already gone into *destroyed* modality. Those wild animals in holiday litter around and smash everything wherever they pass, like a herd of migrating bison.

They say Americans during the Vietnamese war caused death and destruction: it seems to me they are still fighting, but in the wrong place. After their passage I find Iced Tea sadly dropping all over the drinks table, ice cubes mixed in the teabags bowl, teabags on the floor, dirty cups among clean ones, dirty glasses scattered everywhere.

Americans are known as a peaceful people, always with peace by their side; you can understand this from the fact that in almost every war fought on earth, Americans felt the need to be somehow involved; plus, in almost every house there are firearms devoted only to the diffusion of peace. Then, they have never lost a war except than in Vietnam, and now they seek revenge on a cruise: on duty at the buffet I've got this impression. I'm surprised they don't come for breakfast with a rifle on their shoulders.

Angry Waiters   *Federico Fumagalli*

The machines that were once supposed to dispense coffee and tea are in pieces, armchairs have torn leather, some tables have missing legs, acres of fitted carpet in smoking ruins. When they are done with the Battle for Breakfast they put the American flag on the soil: they have conquered the eggs and bacon station, now nothing and nobody can stop them.

There is nothing else left for me to do but to assess the damages, declare the state of emergency and clean up.

Also, the round hole between ice and lemon is just a simple link between the table and the rubbish bin where dirty items are always more than welcome. But it seems that Passengers are scared of this black hole and they don't come any closer.

I try to explain to them that if they throw their tissues inside here, there are no additional charges.

It's impossible to explain to everyone the same thing by voice, reason why my professional mind begins to create a very unprofessional solution. I write it down on a piece of paper and I stick it on the wall, just next to the black hole:

HOW TO USE THE GARBAGE BIN:

1 – Keep the garbage in your hand

2 – Put your hand over the hole

3 – Let the garbage fall down from your hand into the bin

Try! It's not dangerous!

Thank you.
The Management.

When the Head Waiter finds this operational instruction on the wall, I feel like my life has come to an end. He probably did not like it one bit. If he could dissolve me in chlorine, I'm sure he would.

Sometimes cups and glasses run out before I get time to realise it, because the most intelligent ones pick up three glasses each one to avoid getting their ass up from the chair one more time. A lady particularly thirsty impresses me with the amount of liquid she really wants to swallow: three glasses of water, two cups of coffee, two iced tea, one prune juice, one glass of ice, one camomile tea. Now I understand why she looks like a submarine.

I return to my Indian dishwasher friends, who are having fun manually unblocking one of the drains, and I scream: "GLAAASSEEES!! CUUUUPS!! WHAT THE FUUUUUCK!!" and in a nanosecond everything is ready.

That's the way!

COLLECTING DIRTY SILVERWARE

I absolutely need to find an empty Black or Brown box because I have to run around the buffet stations collecting dirty silverware and wash it. After washing it's time to:

DRYING AND COLLECTING (CLEAN) SILVERWARE

This job has to be carried out by two people. The first one (Drying Silverware boy) stays burrowed beside the noisy washing machine for five hours losing his hearing ability and drying heaps of cutlery (I'm talking of about two thousand eight hundred Passengers, not a joke). Also he has to divide them by type.

The Collecting Silverware boy brings the dried cutlery to the lines of the buffet, where comes in action the:

PLATES AND SILVERWARE DISPENSER

They stuck me with two weeks of Supporting Team shift, but we Italians call it Supposting Team. Now, if you are not Italian, you can't understand why we call it that way; I need to explain.

'Supposting' comes from 'Supposta'; *Supposta* is the kind of medicine that the doctor prescribes you when you are sick but you can't swallow it; the one that must be inserted somewhere else to feel better: in English it's *suppository*, I suppose. Well, being in ~~Suppository~~ Supporting Team includes a lot of last-minute changes to the roster, extra *'bull-shi(f)ts'* and lot of broken promises, so we have to take it up our ass anyway. So, *Supposting* is the action slang of 'Push one *Supposta*

Angry Waiters   *Federico Fumagalli*

up in the right place', and since the Team is made of more people, here you go: I am in Supposting Team for two weeks. Will I feel better after two weeks of treatment?

First, the timetable never matches with the one on the message board.

When the ship is sailing, Supposting Team starts at 09.30 and finishes at 14.30; when the ship is standing in port, Supposting Team should work from 06.30 to 09.00 and again (in theory) from 13.00 to 15.00.

It would be too nice to really happen. Now we start to feel the effects of too many Suppostas.

If one week I'm off at Saint Martin (Tuesday, though it's not a day off: maybe a few hours of freedom if I'm lucky, and never after 16.00), at Saint Thomas (Thursday) I work in Donatello dining room from 11.30 to 15.00.

Same story next week: if I work at Saint Martin, I'm off at Saint Thomas.

Off?! What?! There is no such a thing like a day off here. There are NO days off for the whole length of the contract.

However, as soon as I arrive on duty I wait in the corridor behind the lift challenging Head Waiters and colleagues for the *loudest yawn*.

When everybody is there, more or less alive, I carefully listen to the duty they stick me in: "Mr Fredrico: Plates and silver, Starboard side!"

"My name is *not* Fredrico. It's Federico". I want to

Angry Waiters   *Federico Fumagalli*

make it clear.

"Right, that's exactly what I said!"

I don't understand: even if they have my name written in black and white, they never miss to pronounce it wrongly.

I walk to my working post and ask: "What do you want me to do?!" and judging by the face of my colleague I think that finally some good luck is coming my way: my place is behind a table next to the line inside the buffet; what I have to do is to give away plates with cutlery wrapped up in a napkin to the Passengers that come hungrier than ever. My real duty would be 'installing my feet on the ground and not moving any more until the end of my days.'

I have this bad feeling after only half an hour, when my balls are shaking violently in order to keep me awake and alert. Obviously, sometimes I feel the need to scratch them a bit to keep them quiet, but I can't use my hands because they are holding plates and napkins (hygiene first of all), so the only thing I can do is to lean close on the edge of the service table and scrape left and right, up and down. It looks like I am fucking the table, but nobody seems to notice anything. They are all staring at the food and no one is interested in my balls.

After half an hour I can't stand it any more, I'm already annoyed about ☺ing to everyone while asking: "Good morning, Mr Rumenta, good morning, Madame la Putaine (French for 'prostitute'), how are you today?

~80~

Angry Waiters   *Federico Fumagalli*

Here is your plate!"

"Oh, thank you!" – "You're welcome!"

Two thousand eight hundred times.

But I carry on this way, preparing plates and wrapped napkins with spoons knives and forks and ☺s and good mornings and thank yous and you're welcomes.

One hour later: I feel total paranoia, my glance is lost in emptiness, the happiness of tired seaweed, the kindness of a shark.

No... really... I can't manage it any more... My eyelids are closing against my will... Plates, napkins, spoons, knives and forks... Plates napkins, spoons, knives and forks... Plates, nappies, spoons, wives and frogs...

...Teddy bears...

Suddenly I realise that I'm running out of items, for example:

– Plates: "Excuse me, where can I find plates?"

"In the other side of the buffet."

"Where is the other side?"

"... In the other side, no?"

– Knives: "Excuse me *Fre... Fredroco*, where can I find a knife?"

"Stuck into your back, if you call me *Fredroco* again!"

– Forks: "Excuse me, no more forks?"

Angry Waiters   Federico Fumagalli

"And who said that I care?"

– Spoons: "Excuse me, what about spoons?"
"We use them for soups, porridge, coffee..."
"Yes, I know that. I wanted to know where I can find them."
"Then ask me where can you find them, no?"

After four hours I'm about to die out of boredom; it's terribly boring having this lucky shift for two weeks, but my Head Waiters don't notice it, and if they notice, they wouldn't give a brata. Besides, I don't even dare to complain to them; days ago I did something really bad for the company, a true crime against the rules of USPH. I almost killed two thousand eight hundred Passengers with a *peanut pastry*, but I will explain later on.

The only way to let the time pass by is making fun of Passengers by identifying their defects, but one morning is not enough, for us they are all good-for-nothing. And of course, in this job, anything out of the ordinary is an excuse for gossiping.

Sometimes, there's something that makes my head alert, like one day after listening to a man in red short pants who is busy explaining to me all the functions of his remote control (very interesting), I turn my eyes just to see a lady who wants to get a plate with silverware: I am about to land it into her hands, but she has the courage to show me such a ☺ that it could have

Angry Waiters   *Federico Fumagalli*

disarmed half an Iraqi platoon, and I can't do anything but ☺ back at her, my mouth wide open, surprised, without managing to answer 'You're welcome' to her wonderful 'Thanks a million', and I stand there dazed without saying a word until she tugs away the plate from my hands like the python after one month of diet.

Sometimes, I feel so bored that I'd like to answer badly to every useless question; for example I got this lady, around forty years old with make-up, seventy-five without it, who stands *right in front* of the plastic butter containers: she looks around lost in the labyrinth, then she spots me pleading for help: "Excuse me young boy, where is the butter?" I would kindly tell her: 'Would you please get your clothes off, so that I can easily spread you with butter and roll you down the staircase?'

The buffet is completely free of charge and everyone can get anything at any time, but here lies the problem: the Medium American (where for Medium I mean the IQ) takes for granted these words: '*Eat-everything-for-free-always*'.

Sometimes, I find myself staring at hot-air balloons with arms and legs that are scanning the buffet from far away, increasing their paces as if we wanted to keep them out at the very last second; as soon as they come close to me I move away a little bit, fuck knows what happens if one of them stumbled onto me.

Once they reach the food line, they aggressively refill their plates with fried shrimps, pancakes, bacon, omelette, salad, chicken, sweetcorn, onion soup, three dressings, ketchup, mayonnaise, mustard, sushi, cereals, watermelon, pineapple, roast beef, and then they ask me... "Where's the sugar-free dessert?" and on this I go mad, this is too much: 'Go to hell, you and your fuck-free dessert! You are a drain! Don't you see your hugeness? You eat in a day what a tribe of desperate can afford in a month, and you ask for sweetener? And a Diet Coke? WTF?!?'

How about a slice of ass?

TOAST MACHINE

Everyone's nightmare.

Starting in the early morning, still sleepy, two inches from the Toast Machine, is a nightmare. I'm getting baked, literally, maybe I should turn the temperature down a bit, but this would lead to a complaint for not-very-hot-toast, so I have to leave it on 'HIGH'. I feel like I'm on duty in hell, my Supervisor is Satan, but I must stay there, next to this volcano which erupts toasts a go-go for the whole morning. At mid-morning my brain is well and truly gone.

As luck has it, little by little my dear Passengers show up because they need a white toast, brown toast, wheat toast, wholemeal toast, multigrain toast, a bagel for the salmon, an English muffin.

I remember a true gentleman, whose intellect matches with the one of a pillow cover: he arrives, he pulls down his glass and stares at my eyes. I feel uncomfortable, but then I notice that his eyes are looking somewhere else... he is trying to read my name on my name badge, but his eyes are wandering. With one he can look at the stars, with the other he can tell my shoe size. Somehow, he manages to look in the same direction – whichever it is – with both eyes and asks me: "Excuse me, Frendrico, can I have one *skimmed milk*?"

Now, his eyes had played a bad trick: first, I'm not 'Frendrico', but Federico; second... where the hell has he seen the milk? Even I don't know where it is.

I'm not even sure he has actually asked me that, so I ask him to repeat.

"CAN I HAVE ONE SKIMMED MILK?!?"

Apart from the fact that I don't have skimmed nipples, I look at him a bit surprised for his reaction, and I answer kindly that: "I'm sorry, I only make toast here. The milk is in the middle line, just over there (maybe; but I had to get rid of him)." I indicate and point with my finger, to make sure he can see where I'm trying to send him. But he doesn't sound so sure: "Yes, but... Where is the middle?" and that said I raise my eyes to the roof: "My friend, the middle is in the middle, no?"

BOX STATION NUMBER 3

"Mr Fumigayli: Box number 3!"

Angry Waiters   Federico Fumagalli

"My surname is Fumagalli!" I reply.

"Yes, that's exactly what I said: Fumagayli."

"No, you made the same mistake twice: it's Fu-ma-gal-li." I correct him.

Mistake: never correct a Head Waiter.

"Mr Fumigali, you will take care of Box 3 where you are to separate the garbage. Your colleagues will bring you dirty plates, and you'll have to throw away the wastage in different bins: one for Paper, one for Food, one for Napkins, one for Aluminium. If you have Chicken Bones you might need an extra bin, and for that you'll talk to the Segretario. OK? Enjoy the garbage and... ☺!"

"Is there any bin for Head Waiters?" I murmur to myself.

"I heard you, Fumagayli!"

Great: that's what I came on the cruise ship for! Garbage!

At each side of the buffet, starboard and port side, there are three Box Stations: in total there are six. I'm at number three, starboard side. At the rear of the ship there happens to be only one for each side, but in the middle there are two boxes facing each other, at quite a long distance. In the Box Station there is a little door, inside which there is a square shaped space with a shelf on the wall with six drawers. Keeping that behind me, on my left there is the big window from which I can see the ocean, and the four bins. On my right there is the trolley, and in front of me a worktop with a drawer

~86~

and another big shelf inside which I can use to easily hide from Supervisors. Beyond the worktop, I can see the whole dining room area.

First things first: gloves on my hands. If I'm lucky I'm still holding the pair that I've been using for either bread or socks.

While I'm having fun sweeping crap left and right, I have to pile up plates in order of shape: oval, round; bowls and cutlery in the black box; cups go in the brown box.

Sometimes I receive chicken bones, and since I don't have yet neither the extra bin nor the rubbish bag, I fix everything with a professional technique known as 'IDGAF' (I Don't Give A Fuck): I throw bones in all bins, randomly; I don't want to have a headache just because I don't have the proper material to work with.

If I'm lucky there's the 'Collecting plates and cups' guy on duty, but obviously lucky I am never, therefore I need to manage myself running back and forth to my Indian dishwasher friends, without the trolley available for me. Where the hell is the trolley when I'm on duty?! Everyone always has one, but when I'm on, it seems to disappear in some kind of void. Most probably the Indian dishwashers have hidden it away for revenge. Fair enough. One day I kept going in and out to the main switch of their gigantic washing machine to turn it off any time I could, and then I went to complain to a supervisor that their job was too slow. Eventually one of them caught me and complained to the same supervisor. He didn't believe them; hence their hate increased.

Sometimes there are so many Passengers eating that my friendly colleagues bring me piles of plates so tall that I can't see their faces. Also, I have to quicken up my already quick ability of sweeping garbage: paper here, food there, napkins over there... great! Eventually Mr Thai Segretario appears from nowhere to empty my smelly bins and drag them down to Deck 4 for disposal, but in the meanwhile my job stands still: I can't separate anything until he puts back new bags. Why doesn't he come with new bags before he changes the dirty ones?

Sometimes, he comes and tells me that he will be back *soon* with new bags:

"Are you mentally retarded? What am I supposed to do with all this garbage in the meanwhile?"

"You – wait! You – no – worry!" He replies with his broken Thai voice.

"Me – wait, but then – your testicles - I cut! Can't you arrive with new empty bags straight away? You halt my job!"

"Me – garbage take away! Deck 4! After, me – come back and give new bags!"

"Me – your slit eyes – slit apart with knife!"

After two minutes of work at a halt, my plates reach heights that I could climb on them, creating mountains of filth and remains of all kinds.

I must stay there uselessly until Mr Segretario has

Angry Waiters   *Federico Fumagalli*

done his job and smoked his god-damned cigarette, then I can again put my hands ravaging among smeared napkins, buttered aluminium containers, jammed tissues, remains of omelettes, pieces of bacon, mouth-watering second hand toasts, greasy onion soups and many other delicacies.

Very early in the morning, around 06.00 after meeting, I prepare all the necessary stuff and then I go for my breakfast. At 06.30 I come back, and if the buffet line is open – like today, Starboard side – we all start straight away. Slowly, slowly, but straight away.

Otherwise, if Port side is open, then Starboard side would be closed and would open up at 08.00 or 08.30, and I would have to stay inside there doing nothing (really nothing) for two hours: we all understand that we can relax a little bit, and maybe we should be grateful to the management for that, but... why can't we start two hours later? We could easily and happily sleep two extra hours! But maybe at the high positions of management somebody is not happy if we don't work more than necessary. I guess they deal with whips and chains.

The only thing that's left to do for us, the 'Supposting Team – Torture Division', is to sit our butts on some upside-down trays on top of the rubbish bins, waiting for some Passengers to show up, as hungry as sleepy.

I spot the first bunch of them as soon as I come on duty at 05.30; their mouths already watering. Why would they get up so early if they are on vacation?

Angry Waiters   *Federico Fumagalli*

Some just want to admire the rising sun, which seems a reasonable reason even to me. Others instead are to be headbutted instantly, like this gentleman, another true *gentleman* in his fifties with shiny copper hair and another pair of true gentleman's wandering eyes that are looking out through the big windows. I'm still crossing the threshold of the door that leads to the open air Pizzeria, from which I will arrive at Calypso bar and then inside the buffet dining room. I'm walking zigzag, still dazed by the precocious awakening, hands in my pockets, until he suddenly stops me to ask: "Excuse me, where is the sun?"

I open my eyes trying hard to look into his ones, and I make an effort to realise if he is really asking me where the sun is. Maybe I misunderstood because at this time of the morning even shadows play tricks on me, and I'm so sleepy; I try to understand what a M.A. (Medium American) could ask me at 05.30 in the morning, but nothing meaningful comes to my mind. I'd love to ignore him totally, but my sorrowful conscience overcomes me, so I reply apologising: "Sorry?" and he says again: "Where is the sun? And at what time does it come out?".

Oh shit, he really wants to know where the sun would rise... and also at what time.

I know where, but how am I supposed to know the exact time?

Only then I notice that he is holding in his hands the Daughter of the Queen Pattern, the paper that informs

Angry Waiters   *Federico Fumagalli*

all Passengers about everything happening in and out of the ship, from the drink of the day to show performance times and locations; from special offers to horoscopes; from cradle to the grave; from the opening time of the bar to the size of your bra. This paper is printed weekly but distributed daily, because the cruise lasts seven days so every week is always the same story; it contains all the information they need to know; this shiny copper haired true gentleman could find answers to questions that his brain hasn't made up yet, if only he would bother to read it. At that moment I realise why those questions have been made to me rather than having been searched in the DOTQ Pattern: he is a M.A!

However, since I'm almost running late, I decide to ruin his day; who knows if he has sense of humour? I'm going to find out soon enough.

"The sun?" I answer. "It's up there in the sky!" and I ☺, since this is the basic brand standard.

He doesn't really like my brand standard, or maybe his mood is grumpy due to my answer?

"Are you kidding me? I know that! I asked you where I can see it rising!"

'*No, you asked me where it is.*' I think.

He is quite pissed off; I just created an unhappy Passenger. He doesn't have sense of humour. Besides, I suck at jokes, especially at 05.30am.

Knowing that the sun would rise at 06.30 from *this side* of the ship, I tell him that "You have to go *to the other side!"*

After a couple of hours I'm still trenched inside my box; I'm sorting my shit in different bins fast like a bullet train, when a lady calls me: I lift my eyes and I am stunned by her ugliness. She is too ugly to be true; I try hard not to laugh at her face and I listen to her: "What can I do for you, baby?"

I'm ☺ing.

"Can I have a Cheese Omelette?" she says.

'Where the fuck do you see Cheese Omelettes?' I think.

"Cheese Omelettes? Madame, you can find Omelettes in the buffet line, right there." I say, pointing my finger somewhere in the distance, beyond the horizon.

"Oh, really? So what are you doing here? Aren't you cooking?"

'No, Madame: I have a nice of variety of garbage. Fancy a sample?'

The Box is, though it shouldn't be, the meeting point for the ones who want to eat or drink something stolen – or slyly asked – from the buffet or bar. As I said, eating and drinking (even soft drinks) is absolutely forbidden.

I have this feeling that one day I will die starving, if the ship doesn't sink first.

If you are brave enough to eat, just lean down behind the Box's worktop and hope that no Head Waiters or

Angry Waiters　　　　　　　　　　　*Federico Fumagalli*

Supervisors are around, otherwise what you get is a shower of brata on your head.

Indeed, as for the iron rules of USPH (there you go, again) it's strongly forbidden to consume food and beverage in any location of the ship, especially when the ship is standing in American Ports. Or rather, for the Crew is forbidden to eat or drink anywhere for the whole length of the contract.

Working on a ship full of food and feeling starving is like racing in Formula 1 and being told to slow down. It's like being in a room with a bunch of sexy nymphomaniac women and being told you can't touch them.

But rules are made to be broken, or at least interpreted to anyone's will, and since I spot lots of people eating and drinking under the protection of the Turning Guardian – in this case the guardian is the one who works inside the box – I decide to challenge my faith because I'm starving. I walk to the back of the buffet's kitchen near the service lifts, I make sure nobody is looking or coming toward me, I open one of the two fridges and I pick up a couple of pastries with peanuts. With the corner of my eyes I scan around. Nobody has seen me.

How do I open the fridges which are usually locked? With the hook of my wine opener and the spiky pin of my name badge. It even works for some of the locks of the dining rooms.

Triumphant I hide them in the pocket of my green

flowery shirt and go back to my Box number 3. I'm quite proud of my advanced theft skills.

After a few minutes a Head Waiter comes to check that everything is running smoothly, and since everything is Excellent – another brand standard – he nods satisfied with me and walks away to check somewhere else.

As soon as he turns behind the corner I ask Bogdan (a nice guy, tall and large, with the skill of recognising the accent of every American) to ring the alarm bell in case Head Waiters or Supervisors are in sight.

I go down on my knees behind my box, thanking my Guardian.

Unfortunately, my nice Guardian doesn't get the info properly; he gets the information upside down.

Most probably, my English is not good enough to explain to him what I mean.

While I'm on my knees tasting and gulping my second peanut pastry, ☺ing from happiness like a baby holding a teddy bear on his birthday, I raise my eyes just to see the head of a Head Waiter that Bogdan is *purposefully* gone to call for me. He is staring at me in disbelief.

I stare at him in disbelief too.

My heart sinks. My peanut pastry is stuck in my throat.

I'm a dead Junior Waiter.

The Head Waiter is enraged because *I must not* eat behind the box, then he becomes outrageously mad because inside it he finds the Coke of Sakorn and the Sprite of Sukan – whose drinks I didn't know to be there – that the Headwaiter thinks to belong to me, than he brings me to another Head Waiter who starts to scream more shit at me, and who threatens to bring me to the Maître d' if I am caught again, because for USPH rules we risk getting the ship closed down, we stumble into unthinkable troubles, we can be immediately disembarked, Passengers might be contaminated by foreign bacteria and unknown viruses... all these bullshit.

Of course I don't even try to look out for some sort of excuse, because I know I'm perfectly wrong, and I should know that I never ever have to challenge my faith because it is a battle lost in the beginning, but if for a peanut pastry the ship is about to sink, what should us 'Slaves' say about those 'Masters'? We know very well that they have Special Hidey Stations in the pantry of each dining room and behind the Napkin Folding station. Those are hidden areas, but still near Dining Areas, close to the Passengers always fooling around, with high chances for them to spot these mysterious places and see something that they have never seen before: 'Oh my god! A Waiter is *eating*!'

So why are Head Waiters and Supervisors allowed to fuck around with the rules, and we get the shit? Don't they risk contaminating Passengers as well?

If in the Clean Areas *nobody* is allowed to eat and

Angry Waiters   *Federico Fumagalli*

drink at *any time* of the day, why is *somebody* allowed?

"Mr Frenderic! No-More-Peanut-Pastries until the end of your life, OK? Keep hungry, keep employed!" is what they tell me.

'My name is not Fren…' I'd like to say, but I save it. "Never mind".

OK. Despite my name pronounced wrongly again, I got the lesson.

No-More-Peanut-Pastries.

I go back to my box, stomach rumbling.

Another grin on my face. Lesson taught, my ass.

They didn't say 'No more strawberry tartlets'.

I'm already on my way to the pastry fridge.

At the end of the shift, one of the two followings things could happen:

1: I could be Lucky

2: I could be Unlucky

If I am Lucky – almost never – my working line is open and Passengers can go on shamelessly sponging plates and littering them with food, from which I have to sort out the respective debris. Today, my line is again on Starboard side. We never ever remember which side is which, so the trick is: "You have to count the letters that form the words: Port is four letters, exactly like Left; Starboard is nine letters, *not exactly like* Right, which is five, but keep in mind Port, and you will remember! Understand?" The Head Waiter

Angry Waiters   *Federico Fumagalli*

tells us.

"Yeeeaaah!" We all shout like sheep.

"Then go! What are you waiting for?"

I walk to him.

"So... I am in starboard side, right?" I ask.

"Exactly, Fumagayli, and starboard side is... you know which side?"

"Mmm... *left* side?"

"Right side! Fumigayli! Right side! Still you don't get it?! Do you have Alzheimer or what?!"

"Actually, I'm not even Fumagayli, nor Fumigali, nor whatever you keep calling me..."

At 11.30 it is time for changing shift: the ones on duty in Lido Lunch come in, and I can go away following the rule of the Head Waiter which says: "You have to leave your Box exactly as you found it in the morning!"

Since in the morning I always find the Box in a pitiful condition, I'm quite happy to walk away without clearing anything, leaving on the shelf mountain of plates so close to shatter on the floor because of their unbalanced position.

Instead, if I am Unlucky – all the other times – the line is shut down and I have to clean from the beginning. Everything must disappear from the Box, and not a single stain or an invisible breadcrumb is admitted by the Head Waiter's control, because though the stain is invisible to the human eye, for the Head

Angry Waiters   *Federico Fumagalli*

Waiter the stain *is still there* and I have to wipe it away, pretending to have understood where the hell it is. I don't want to get a Warning for an invisible stain.

My new weapons are a white bucket filled with water and Chlorine and one Blue Towel. On my hands there are two new latex gloves: with my Cleaning Kit I start to Sanitise everywhere.

Sanitise, sanitise and sanitise, I must disinfect drawers, garbage bins, tiles, glasses, the floor, everything. It's a big pain in the butt, but after having fought the Battle against Bacteria, I can finally and peacefully get the hell out of there. I smell of Chlorine.

But this job is nothing compared to what I have to do when I am on duty:

CLEANING TABLES

…where the sanitising has to be done at the end of the shift. I have to sanitise all tables, chairs, pedestals, and most terrific: pass the brush on the floor. We call the brush 'Scopetta', because in Italian we call it 'Scopa', and the action verb is 'Scopare'.

Scopetta is a small brush.

Now: 'Scopare' in Italian has two meanings: the first one is 'to brush the floor', for example before mopping; the second is 'To Fuck – Having Sex'.

I have to brush the floor.

The use of Scopetta on the floor is deadly terrible because the floor is carpeted: square miles of fitted

~98~

carpet and no matter how hard are my efforts to brush it, the crumbs jump left and right and everywhere, except inside the scoop. I would go faster by picking them up one by one with my fingers.

And of course every single point touchable with hand and visible with eye has to be sanitised.

This is the end of the shift of Cleaning Tables. What might I have to do *before* the service? Exactly the same, because the lazy night workers never do what they are supposed to do. I'm sanitising 24/7.

Armed once again with bucket and Blue Towel (if I can find it, because sometimes there are not enough of them for everybody, and I have to steal one from the chefs with new subterfuges that I learn with time) I start to sanitise from early morning, my nose getting Chlorine vapours inside.

My eyes also fall on the sugar containers, just waiting to be refilled.

Slowly slowly Passengers appear, and hiding my Blue Towel in the pocket of my green flowery shirt, I start going back and forth to my station checking continuously for empty plates to collect. If there are plates, the agony begins: "Excuse me, did you finish? Did you enjoy it? Can I take it away (referring to the plate)?", "Yes, thank you", "You're welcome".

Two thousand eight hundred times.

After an hour my guts have had enough of answering You're Welcome endlessly; other than that, many times a single Passenger tells me "Thank you" up to

Angry Waiters   *Federico Fumagalli*

four times in the same occasion.

Now, mathematics has always been my enemy, but:

2800 Thank yous

× 4

= 11200 You're Welcomes.

You try and tell me.

And that's only for the morning shift! I have another shift in the dining room in the evening! Seven or eight more hours of Thank yous and You're Welcomes! Thousands! Gazillions of them!

For example, I get to the table and I ask if I can clear the plates: "Yes, Thank you." – "You're Welcome." I take the plate, and then I collect the cutlery left on the table (they should stay on the plate when the guest is done with the meal, but thy are Americans: what do they know about food etiquette?): "Thank You." – "You're Welcome." But then I spot some empty sugar sachets, and I have to pick them up: "Thank You." – "You're Welcome."

I'm about to go away, but my eye catches the empty glass that the other friend has just rushed to finish. Should I leave it on the table? Of course not, so my hand moves once again: "I'm sorry…" I take it. And one more time: "Thank You." – "YOU'RE WELCOOOOOOOME!!!!!"

Cleaning tables back and forth I have all the time to study the M.A: the intelligence of these people is impressive; their habits are always new and

Angry Waiters   *Federico Fumagalli*

imaginative; their behaviour allows me to connect the Man to the Beast, especially in the dining area, because the M.A. doesn't know how to behave at a dining table.

It's the case of this Starving Lady with curly blonde hair in front and plain red behind, which shows me that her brain is tuned on a mysterious frequency: she is not the one with abnormal tonnage, she fits the average of one hundred and ten kilograms.

Starving Lady reaches the buffet at 11.00, refilling two plates with so much food that she could feed a kindergarten, and she sits on the screaming armchair. At 11.02 she orders a *Diet* Coke (of course). I check that her Cruise Card had the Red Sticker on it and I walk to the bar to get her drink.

11.07: Starving Lady has already sucked up the whole iced drink, ice cubes included. At 11.10, disaster: she leans on the right side of the table, bends down, and vomits whatever was inside her voracious belly. She vomits on the carpeted floor, a symphony of colours and guttural rumbling all around; I can even spot the Diet Coke's bubbles.

It's the end of the world.

If we have been careful during Inductions, we should know what to do in case of vomit: the sick person has to be kept still where he is (she, in this case), and she is not allowed to go anywhere. We have to call the Head Waiter or Supervisor or whoever is in charge, who will then call the experts in vomit cleaning, the Disinfection Team. We also must close the infected line for at least two hours and leave the Disinfection Team to have fun.

It looks like we have been invaded by aliens: men in white suits, white shoes, white gloves, face masks, measuring instruments, stethoscopes and all sorts of gadgets. I wouldn't be surprised if they'd landed on board riding a flying Smart car.

While these guys are fighting the Battle against Vomit, Starving Lady gets a medical check by Astrodoctors to find out what had caused her sickness. My diagnosis is 'Excess of Food and Iced Diet Coke', but to Astrodoctors and zoologists it would take ages of checks and biological examinations to find out what kind of bacteria has to be blamed. The only real bacteria, as per my useless opinion, is her brain.

The whole Starboard side line gets shut down, and all Passengers have to be moved more or less kindly to the other side of the buffet, all of them to Port side. I fear a sudden capsize of the ship. The danger of me dying sinking is more real as each day passes by.

This sudden change of plan in the line creates a giant Brata, because the people in excess have to gather in heaps with the others already eating. And usually nobody seems too keen about making up some space: one person sitting alone takes space for six, since most of the tables are for four or six people. There is just not enough space, because Medium Americans don't cooperate between themselves. There is a drama? They get a table and that's it: no sharing with others. They

Angry Waiters   *Federico Fumagalli*

put bags and newspapers all over the seats, and don't have a care in the world.

11.30: Starving Lady feels better, but I can hear her stomach crying out for food. She gets up and moves toward the buffet. We all scan her, alert and worried, until she comes out with one only plate, either half full or half empty. Our blood pressure calms down.

I go back to work, waiting for the Lunch Team to come and replace me and the others from the morning.

11.31: Starving Lady stretches out from her new table and vomits one more time on the clean carpeted floor, in the new operating line. I put hands on my face.

At this point all our hopes vanish, we have to close the second line for two hours, which means that until 13.30 nobody is allowed to eat on the Horizon Court buffet on the Deck 14, in its entirety.

We ☺ at each other: we have to send everybody down to the dining room, where it's usually not very busy, and nobody down there has a clue of what a massive brata they are going to drown in.

Our Head Waiter goes to talk to Starving Lady, before the Astrodoctors have the chance to return and send her back to Planet Idiot. He tells her: "Madame, if tomorrow morning you feel like throwing up again, why don't you come at 7am so we close early and we all get back to sleep?"

11.33 I finally finish Lido Breakfast shift and I go down to the Crew Mess to eat. I'm already tired, I need to sleep, and the food sucks. I try to put a remedy on

Angry Waiters   *Federico Fumagalli*

its taste by shaking a lot of salt and pepper on the food. Then I go to the Drinks Machine, I pull out my Crew Cash Card and I slip it into the appropriate slot. I have credit on it, around twenty dollars, so I press the button for Fanta – the Queen of all drinks – but the machine runs out empty. Fuck it, no more Fanta, the only thing that gives me a good mood at lunch, and I have to go to the second Drinks Machine which is located in the Officer's Staff Room. I try my luck and... this bloody machine doesn't even read my card. WTF!

More and more disgusted I go to the juice machine for a glass of orange juice, which has obviously run out of orange, whose juice falls down with a kind of yellow-with-fever colour.

My last chance is a glass of disgusting water that tastes of Chlorine.

After eating I'm amok, so I try to call home, in Cremella. I walk up to the phone room, designated to satisfy the exigencies of one thousand two hundred Proud Crew Members; the sick mind of the Creator must have stopped at an age between Palaeolithic and Paralytic: who can be so dumb to install only four telephones?!

Everyone knows that intercontinental calls are always long, and that for this reason the queue at the phones is always kilometric! Indeed: the queue I have in front of me, from out the door, doesn't even allow me to see the phones.

I roar.

Angry Waiters   *Federico Fumagalli*

OK, it's not possible to make a call, I see if I can at least connect to the Internet. I walk all the long way of the ship – Crew Mess with Phone Rooms is on the stern (the ass); the computer room is in the Crew Bar, on the bow, Deck 8. I enter the internet room, and today my lucky star is a fallen star: five PCs available and only one is working but somebody else got it already. I wait half an hour during which I keep yawning noisily until the guy on the PC gets the message and runs away. Nobody else around, PC is mine!

I connect, I enter my e-mail address, and as by magic... the PC dies in front of me. Shut down. Forever.

I stare at it, unsure about smashing it or not on the face of somebody, but unfortunately there is nobody, then I calm down and I go back to my grave.

On the way back I think that nobody asked me to come here, I did it intentionally.

I am the only one to blame.

I enter my microscopic cabin, and I decide to wash my socks; I take from my pocket the latex gloves which I use to pick up the Passenger's bread; it takes me around half an hour, due to the cappuccino cup size sink. Also, the glove is not the best thing I could use to stop the water from going down, so I have to keep the tap running, and add some more detergent, or Chlorine. Honestly, I have already had enough of Chlorine.

After that the only other important thing I have to do is to put my head down for a couple of hours or less. I switch on 'The Cold White Light' by Sentenced in my CD player and skip until the last song, 'No one there'. I have to listen to it with earphones, but I leave them on the small shelf behind my head, so I can hear just a muffled relaxing sound. I set the alarm for about 16.00, now it's just 14.00 and…

Zzz…

14.20: one of the two Thai gays that share the bathroom with me, but stay in the room opposite the bathroom – I mean the bathroom is between the two cabins – arrives after his shift for a shower, managing to make lot of noise because the door is everything but soundproof. I can even hear when he moves the curtain, and I don't want to say anything about what I can hear when the two heroes take a shower together.

He is keeping me awake, and I have been sleeping only twenty minutes.

14.40: he is still under the shower, singing the Thai National Anthem.

Rrrr…

I get up and I knock with a moderate manner to let him know that he is pissing me off big time. He understands, and goes back in his room.

I put my head down again.

14.55: the Mexican who lives in the cabin opposite my wall, front side of my bed, arrives in his room and switches on his own stereo. I can't hear his music, but I am annoyed by the powerful bass system: it's so

Angry Waiters   *Federico Fumagalli*

powerful that I can feel the walls shaking and bouncing. This is not the first time that he plays this trick on me, so I get up again, crawling to the end of my bed, and I kick the wall for two minutes until I hear somebody knocking on my door: I open it and I find the girl in the opposite room – the room on my right – screaming at me because I woke her up by kicking the wall of another room.

Rrrrrr…

Any explanation is useless for an idiot like her; she doesn't even want to understand that the fucking noise is coming out from the opposite room. I show her the signs I left in the plastic panel on the wall I've been kicking and she calms down, but at the same time, who does arrive? Mr Jesus, the Mexican, to ask me if I can stop beating the wall otherwise he can't listen to his music.

WHAT'S WRONG WITH THESE PEOPLE?!

I'm going insane, the lady is screaming, the guy is shouting; I grab his arm and I drag him inside to show him the noise of his bloody bass sound Latin dance disco music, I explain that I want to sleep, but the girl comes in to tell me that if I want to sleep I shouldn't be kicking the wall, and this makes me angry, I threaten to kick her chubby ass as I did the wall, lady or not, my eyes are red, sparking both fury and Chlorine, she understands and disappears quickly like a cartoon.

The Mexican does the same, on the other hand I don't want somebody called Jesus in my room, I'm atheist

Angry Waiters   *Federico Fumagalli*

and totally against any kind of religion, especially Christian, and in a few seconds the stereo goes dead.

I don't hear anything else, just my heartbeat and the bathroom vent, not to say anything about that strange droning noise that I can't identify, coming from somewhere. Eventually, I manage to fall asleep.

I am so tired that I don't hear the alarm at 16.00.

I eventually open my eyes when my room-mate Robert goes out shutting the door. I haven't even heard him coming in.

I'm so dazed and sleepy that I can't figure out if I have to get changed for Breakfast or for Dinner. After a while of mental confusion I get to the conclusion that the night before we had the Galley Round, so I must now wear the Breakfast uniform.

It's so nice to possess such a phenomenal intuition.

As I enter the dining room I realise my breathtaking mistake: from the windows comes the light of the sun (in my cabin I don't have windows), and as my colleagues see me, they begin slagging me as much as possible.

I run like crazy back to my cabin, I change as fast as I can, changing the buttons from one uniform to another (why don't they give us all uniforms complete with buttons? Why do we have to unbutton one uniform and button up the other one?), I fly back once again in the dining room at 16.50, twenty dangerous minutes late and a catastrophic feeling burning inside me: indeed, at my station *everything* is missing. After

Angry Waiters   *Federico Fumagalli*

slagging me they have stolen twelve water glasses, eight wine glasses, two chairs, and two water jugs. They could have conquered the whole station.

I'm very pissed off, the beast arises… they want war? Good… I take care of remembering all these little things, for another occasion, not very far away…

I quickly set-up what I have to set-up, my waiter is not here yet, at least I don't get complaints from an idiot that would shout rather than help.

I get back almost everything I've lost, go in the Galley to fill up water jugs and ice bucket, and when I get back to the station there is something else missing, this time from the tables, and that is even more unfair, we all agreed not to steal from already set-up tables, yet somebody has broken the rules. I mutter to break bones, keep on cursing loudly, pray that SARS take them one by one, until a Head Waiter calls me at 17.16 for the meeting in Bernini dining room – I'm one minute late – and I sit down.

I still have six more hours to go, and this automatically puts my energy down by ninety per cent.

Angry Waiters   *Federico Fumagalli*

~~11~~
LIDO LUNCH

Exactly as with Lido Breakfast, the routine is the same with the only difference being the time: at 11.15 there is the usual meeting and at 11.30 the show begins.

Does being on duty in Lido Lunch mean that we can sleep a little bit more? Not always. Indeed, if I'm not on duty for some Induction at 09.00, I run the risk of stumbling into the Bow Drill at 09.45, always on Tuesday when we are in Saint Martin. I never remember if the correct name of this island is Saint Maarten or Saint Martin.

If there are no pain-in-the-arse duties I could sleep until 10.30 and then have my lunch, though it's not so pleasurable having it at breakfast time.

But anyway I like to have a nice breakfast whenever is possible, so if I wake up in possession of all my abilities, like walking straight without bouncing against the walls, at 09.00 I'm in the Crew Mess to eat, unless I feel really dead. In this case I get up at the very last minute, allowing me just enough time to shower, shave and cover eventual cuts on my face due to my old razor. Last time I changed the blade was four weeks ago; maybe I should get a new one, since I have to shave my ugly face every single miserable morning. I look like a ~~scarecrew~~ scarecrow.

I eat from the pasture what is left for the livestock and I begin working non-stop until night. There should be

~110~

Angry Waiters   *Federico Fumagalli*

a break between 16.00 and 16.30: the shift ends at 16.00 and the next shift in the dining room is about 16.30, but counting the length of time waiting for the lift, getting down, walking all the way along to my cabin, I lose around seven minutes. If the shower is not taken by somebody else, I can make it in five minutes, five minutes to get dried, dressed, sorted out, change the buttons to the new uniform, prepare the dirty linen to be washed by my Filipino, at 16.29 I have to go back to the dining room, and my break is well and gone to hell.

During Lido Lunch on the buffet I grab the chance to study the Medium American.

Whilst Cleaning Tables, I walk back and forth between my tables to clear away dirty plates and to watch the boobs of the girls in swimwear. But even so, time passes slowly, especially when the ship is docking in some port.

I repeat that the whole Crew is of the opinion that the M.A, besides being a Cippettone (the one who doesn't tip), is also feeble-minded. I mean: you, M.A, come to this island once in a lifetime, and you stay on board for lunch, eating on the buffet or in the dining room admiring the wonderful view that you wanted so much to see – and we can't – because we have to stay on board for You… oh idiot! Why don't you move your ass and go out to see yourself your fucking wonderful view?! Go to the beach and get your face tanned! There are plenty of typical restaurants who are waiting to

Angry Waiters   Federico Fumagalli

cook for you the specialty of the place! Get a multi-sandwich and choke on the beach! Eat in the park picnic style! There are restaurants with veranda outside for your wonderful view, or air-conditioned if you want to stay inside… go, please, go! But don't rub it in by telling us "Oh, what a pity you can't go down under the sun! I'm going for some jet-skiing, later on!" and ☺ing like a fool. I hope a shark crunches your balls!

Some M.A. are capable of getting off the ship in the morning, coming back at midday to eat free of charge at the buffet, then go out again only to definitely come back at 17.00, time for the ship to move away.

Don't they realise that they are wasting their time? Go and lay down on some hammock between palm trees! Hopefully a coconut will smash on your forehead!

A colleague, talking with some Passengers in the morning, asks them: "Why do you come so early at the buffet, while you could sleep a little bit more since you are on vacation?"

The answer is: "Otherwise we don't have time to have breakfast in the dining room *too*!"

It seems they are starving to death, and each passing day makes my mind up on this even more. Here they take advantage of everything they can, they refill their plates with every single possible thing, coating it with six different sauces so that pasta tastes like chicken and the omelette tastes like wild boar.

And then, maybe, they waste half of what they have

taken because they are full of Diet Coke thinking they won't get fat. But they do it so they have wonderful tales to tell their grandchildren. They will show off big time to their neighbours.

Their intuitive powers are also affected, as it happens to this centenarian lady: "Excuse me, is this the table where I sat yesterday?"

"Madame, I can't even remember with whom I slept last night!" (the answer is always 'with *nobody*').

At the buffet all seats are free for everybody, so everyone can choose to sit anywhere they like; we don't take reservations, and we don't remember where somebody is sitting because the turnaround is fast and various. But this absent-minded lady with two centimetres of lipstick seems not to know what is going on. She is unlucky; I'm in a very bad mood because today I lost my precious wine opener and because I missed my lunch (spoiler: my wine opener was actually on my bed, I found it in the evening).

She comes to ask me: "Excuse me, where is my table?" – "How the hell am I supposed to know?!" I reply, and then I turn direction going for a while *to the other side*.

The worst are the ones with Money, taking part in the category M.H.A. (Medium High American) and I realise it when we start the prestigious *Free Sundae* service.

Angry Waiters   *Federico Fumagalli*

~~12~~
FREE SUNDAE

The Sundae is like an ice cream, the same you would find in McDonalds, and in Italy I think I have never seen it anywhere. I don't really know the difference between Ice cream and Sundae, and honestly I couldn't care less. I'm a professional, my own way.

Surprisingly, I find out that this Sundae tastes wonderful. Finally, one score in favour of the cruise ship. But: can I get a scoop or two before starting the shift?

"Of course *not*! If I catch you licking Sundae *again*, I will lick you myself! And now, go! ☺!" shouts at me the Head Waiter, the same one who gave me the warning for the peanut pastry.

Anyway, this Sundae is absolutely free of charge for one hour, for all the people who can manage to get in the queue.

At 15.00 the big sign 'Create Your Own Free Sundae from 15.00 to 16.00' materialises and I am called on duty to take part. On this occasion I am the assistant of Bogdan, the smart guy who called the Head Waiter that gave me a warning; his hands are big enough to squeeze to death a cow. Usually he scoops up the chocolate flavour, leaving to me the vanilla one. There are only two flavours available, then, when the brata hits the fan, Bogdan scratches the two Sundae containers with his steel scoop, and I take care of

~114~

Angry Waiters   *Federico Fumagalli*

squeezing the two available sauces: chocolate and strawberry. The only effort Passengers might have to make is to sprinkle their Sundae with candies.

By themselves.

Next to the buffet's corridor we have to set a two metre long table that, for lack of space, gets almost stuck between the divisor wall of tables and the buffet line, and this wall is not plain straight, but has the shape of sea waves. Though I'm thin like the broth they serve to sick elders in hospital, I can barely move from inside, and I keep scratching my ass on the rough surface.

Bogdan on my left side armed with his scoop, me on the right side holding the Molotov of sweet gravy. If I am Lucky – almost never – everything goes smoothly and accordingly to plan. If I am Unlucky – all the other times – the cylinder that should hold the bottle's neck and the lid of it, at the point where the bottle gets larger, soon or later it tears off and it smears my whole section with very sticky and gummy sauce, ruining all the paper cups, napkins, plastic spoons, etc... It happened with the chocolate sauce, once, and my section really looked like it was covered in – guess what?

One minute to 15.00 and the people are gathering heavily around our shoulders, we can feel their breath on our necks. They are hungry for Sundae. They look like the living dead, shaking hands in motion, asking for Sundae as if it was the last thing they would do in

Angry Waiters   *Federico Fumagalli*

life; their eyes are staring blindly to our Sundae containers. I'd love to dig a finger in the box and lick it in front of everybody, but they would bite my finger off instantly.

The M.H.A. would lose his place in the swimming pool for a free Sundae; he would lose thirty minutes of waiting for two minutes of licking, and I'm still talking about Sundae; he would grab the child before him and throw it at sea.

M.H.A: why don't you go to the deck's bar to get an enormous ice cream, a thousand flavours for two dollars ninety-five cents without getting in the queue, and take advantage of this to cheat with the lady behind the counter who feels so lonely? She needs *you*!

During those sixty minutes I have to make happy three thousand Passengers, because some of them get in the queue twice, but I still manage to study them like an anthropologist, careful to catch their dreams and worries. The major worry is their diet; their biggest dream is to eat the impossible without doubling their belly. Obviously that's not possible, but the M.A. tries anyway to lose weight eating in a day as much as a herd of sharks would do in a week.

I'm so busy saucing left and right, when a lady as skinny as one raw spaghetto (Italian male singular) asks me: "Excuse me, do you have a Sugar Free Sundae?" She looks down in our containers, scanning thoroughly for hints of sugar. I think '*Now that you are not staring at me, is the perfect moment to smash a tray on your face!*', but I say: "Sorry Madame, the Sundae is already Money Free!"

She doesn't get the joke. "I know, but don't you have maybe any Low Fat?"

'*Listen up, wingless chicken…*' but I'm too kind to tell her, so I eventually reply: "Not here, but you can try on the Ice Cream Bar. They charge just two dollars ninety-five cents!" But at the sound of the word 'Charge' she changes her mind. "No, no, OK, I'll take this."

'*You know what you should take more often?*' I ☺. "Follow the line, please."

After a while she reappears in front of me. She orders:

– A little vanilla ice cream
– A little chocolate ice cream
– An enormous coating of both sauces on both ice creams.

'*I thought you wanted a sugar free Sundae! Your brain is as useless as a tampon for a woman who doesn't have her period! I mean: you have it, but what for?!?* ' I think, handing her the healthy Sundae. "Hope you are happy now." I ☺, since this is the King of all brand standards, including the always appropriate 'Excellent!'

But as I said, the worst are the richest: the ones that in the afternoon take lunch for free at the buffet with swim gear and slippers, and at the Gala Dinner they turn up dressing elegantly with suite make up; *they* are

Angry Waiters   *Federico Fumagalli*

the ones who fight with children in the afternoon for a place ahead in the queue for the free Sundae, challenging the kids with plastic spoons, and in the evening in the elegant dining room they scrutinise the wine list like experts, reading it over and over as if the champagne's price would decrease a bit each time, and then they all order Chardonnay Fetzer – eighteen dollars – the most Cippettone on the list; *they* are the ones that once at the Sundae station ask:

– "A cup of vanilla for me"

– "A cup of chocolate for my wife (which usually stands behind him)"

– "A cup with one scoop of vanilla and two of chocolate, with strawberry sauce"

– "A cup with one scoop of chocolate and two of vanilla with chocolate sauce on the vanilla and strawberry sauce on chocolate, and candy all around them, please. Thanks… Fre… Fredric...o?"

"Fe-de-ri-co. There is no R between F and E." I explain. But then I remember that they are reading at my name badge, which wrongly says Frederico, so they aren't so wrong after all.

"Where are you from, Frederico?"

"Italy".

"Ah! Bon Jour!"

"Jesus Christ go away!"

But then, in the evening in the dining room they can't distinguish a pasta from a filet mignon, they eat seafood salad with decaf coffee and they order lobsters

Angry Waiters   *Federico Fumagalli*

with diet coke. Disgusting.

Someone makes the queue up to three times to avoid spending the two dollars ninety-five cents for a mega ice cream topped with ten sauces and biscuits, whipped cream, served in a *crystal* glass and drowned in coffee. I feel pity for them, sometimes I'd like to bring them myself to the bar and offer ice creams a go-go, but then this feeling disappears as quickly as it comes: all I'd give them is a vegan cone.

Just before 16.00, Bogdan and I had better start to put everything away because at 16.00 on the hour we must get off duty and clear out quickly, and under the Passenger's terrified eyes I hear deadly screams and I notice hundreds of fingers flying towards our half empty Sundae's containers, in the vain attempt to pick up the last lumps that they couldn't afford to get.

If I can manage to steal it and bring it in the back of the kitchen, I do it; otherwise I have to run like a hunting dog to my cabin for a shower, change of uniform, and get to whatsoever dining room I have to be.

But today I really want some chocolate Sundae, and… hey… just a moment: here I only have the vanilla container. Where's the other one, the chocolate one? Where's Bogdan?

I come out and go back to the small station; my eyes light up: there you go! The chocolate container! It's almost empty; there might be the last two scoops inside. Bogdan left it there and disappeared.

~119~

Angry Waiters   *Federico Fumagalli*

'*Today is my lucky day!*' I think and smiiiiile☺.

I grab it, reaching for the door that leads to the kitchen, plastic spoon hungrily held in my hand like Thor's hammer.

I don't have the time to open the door when I hear someone calling me.

I have to stop. '*Never* say *No!*' is another of our Brand Standards.

There's a young father who is holding a little monster in pink in his arms. The man points his fingers toward my chocolate Sundae. My heart sinks.

I have to do something before he opens his mouth, maybe I can press the button of the general fire alarm and run away, but there is no such button in the near surrounding, and I can't disappear inside the doors because he would stop me.

Indeed, he makes the I'm-so-sorry face and looks at the half asleep gremlin he is holding. I suddenly understand that he wants to give the Sundae to her, and he needs *my* help to make her happy. Her sleepy eyes make her look like a sorcerer, with the power to make my sundae disappear. I can't let it happen!

What can I do?! What can I do?! This could be my lunch! I need energy! But…

"Excuse me… I see that you still have some ice cream left inside there… for my baby…"

'*Sorry, I don't speak English…*' I want to reply, but I can't.

These are *my* last two scoops! They belong to *me*!

~120~

Angry Waiters   *Federico Fumagalli*

They are *mine*! And *'That baby is way too small to be eating ice cream!'*

"Hummm…" I mutter, twisting my nose.

The poor father is waiting for me to give him some sort of charity, but though I'm totally against about giving away my ice cream, a scary signal appears.

From my back and toward my face, passing over my shoulders, there is a ghost cup moving. Around the cup there is a ghost hand, and a ghost arm.

I realise that it's not a ghost: behind me there is a *real* Head Waiter who kindly and smiling is handing a cup for this gentleman who just wants to make his daughter happy. I ☺ too. Fake, but smile ☹. The voice of the Head Waiter is soft, he murmurs to me: "Where were you thinking to go?"

I can't lie to him. My honest answer, low tone, is: "I was going to clean the plastic scoop so that I could give this gentleman *the last, the very last, after these no more*, two scoops of delicious chocolate Sundae because, as you can see, the plastic scoop is dirty."

"Good boy! Carry on!" he replies. "And… I'm watching you!"

The man is so happy, and walks away with *my* ice cream.

Damn I'm so upset!

I better run to my cabin and change uniform.

On my way back I bump into Bogdan, who is holding a cup full of chocolate ice cream.

"Where the f**k did you get that?"

Angry Waiters   *Federico Fumagalli*

"I asked the Head Waiter."

"I SO MUCH want to set you both on fire..."

But when I'm on duty in Lido Lunch, besides working non-stop, there are other pain-in-the-ass duties, such as:

– Napkin Folding
– Island Night
– Champagne Waterfall

Angry Waiters   *Federico Fumagalli*

~~13~~
NAPKIN FOLDING

After dinner service I have all the time I want for eating, but: I have to crawl up again to the Horizon Court, Deck 14. I have to reach the Napkin Folding station and fold heaps of napkins – usually three big wooden boxes – inside which I put fork, knife and spoon. I have to sit there, waiting to get a severe back pain due to the very uncomfortable chair. Then, around 01:00am I can go away.

These are the napkins with the cutlery I use when I'm in Supposting Team duty.

If I want, I can also avoid doing this job: how? I just have to pay fifteen dollars to somebody else who might strongly need them. There is always somebody available to work for an extra fifteen dollars, and that person is hardly me. I'm the idiot who always pay other smarter idiots.

When I am on Napkin Folding duty, the following day I can start working one hour later, at 12.30, because on the night before I have finished much later: sounds great to me.

Or at least that's what I thought. Just because it's a great thing, it's time to scan for eventual surprises. And there you go: if I start later on because I finish later, isn't it strange that in the afternoon I will finish at 17.00 (instead of 16.00) with the obligation of being on duty in the dining room at 16.30? How can this

Angry Waiters   *Federico Fumagalli*

happen?

I know I shouldn't complain; maybe I am the one who always sees everything wrong, and as usual the ones to be right are *them*.

And so on, keep folding a napkin with fork, knife, spoon; fork, knife, spoon; fork, knife, spoon; pork, wife, broom…

~~14~~
ISLAND NIGHT

How beautiful is to do a whole week of Lido Lunch: I work *only* twelve hours without break, except for the rare times when luck is by my side: by which I mean my lunch at 10.45, and my likely dinner after 23.00.

And how wonderful is the night when we leave Saint Thomas; at 22.45, in theory, I should have already done the following things: already finished work; already finished eating; already walked along the length of the ship to change my uniform in my micro-cabin; already reappeared in Canaletto disguised as Horizon Court. There is nothing better, after a long, heavy and stressful working day without food and water, than having to go back to the buffet to work until midnight.

Again. Once more.

During Island Night we just do the same things we have done for the whole day in Lido Lunch, but more people are needed because of the shows on the deck; also some of us have to prepare Bananas Flambé. I usually Flambé My Banana, but that's another story.

The difference of emotion in this shift is that at this stage I'm dead, so tired, my legs are just painful, I'm so unwilling, my eyes are shutting down automatically, I'm in a dangerous mood, I'd send anybody to hell, and watching the same faces eating again after dinner makes me sick. But this is my job, and as every professional waiter must do, I must fake smiles and courtesy.

Some Japanese Passengers that I got at my station for one whole week, seeing me up in the buffet during Island Night, stop and ask me: "Fedelico san, are you still working?"

At least they can pronounce my name almost properly. It took me four days to teach them, but I appreciate the effort.

"How about you? Are you still eating?!"

There were sixteen of them on a big table at my station in the dining room, ten adults and six kids, ordering tanks of iced tea and avalanches of chocolate milkshakes, and then they disappeared without leaving a dollar tip.

Those are the things that madden us: working like donkeys for a week, and nothing paid back. Luckily, after one week, we will never meet them any more. Not even by mistake.

Or maybe yes?

~~15~~
CHAMPAGNE WATERFALL

This is one of the most awaited events – for the Passengers only, of course: simply knowing that they will be drinking Champagne for free, they get more excited than having a good fuck. Champagne Waterfall beats Baked Alaska and sex.

I must be honest: taking part in the Champagne Waterfall is quite a nice occasion, and it is well organised: there's nice scenery; there's dancing; there's eating and drinking for free (again); there's music; lots of sexy women, and with a little bit of luck you could even go up the long staircase that leads you to the top of the massive pyramid made of glasses, and pour down a real waterfall of champagne, creating hills of vanishing foam. Passengers are enthusiastic about this exhibition, unconscious that what they will drink is not Dom Perignon, but very cheap sparkling wine.

"How much do you think each of these bottles cost?' A Head Waiter asks us.

"Fifteen dollars!"

"No!"

"Twenty-five dollars!"

"No!"

"Forty dollars!"

"No!"

"One hundred and fifty dollars!" We try to guess.

"Congratulations! You are a bunch of morons! Do

Angry Waiters   *Federico Fumagalli*

you really think we would spend *so much as fifteen dollars* per bottle just to see them wasted by those fat-asses? The price of each bottle is *less than one dollar*."

Fair enough.

Thinking about that, it makes sense. Bottles are truly wasted. Champagne gushes from the top filling the glasses underneath.

If all goes well, the lucky VIP on top of the ladder pours the first bottle in the top glass of the pyramid and everything begins to sparkle, cameras begin to flash and mouths begin to cheer: let the party begin! Happy until the end!

But not today.

No, boy: today no happy ending.

A very excited woman in high heels climbs the ladder where the Maître d' is waiting to explain to her the correct technique to pour champagne.

Even Peppa Pig knows that champagne has to be poured slowly slowly, keeping the bottle as still as possible.

But not this lady: with a shaky hand and the intention to impress, she unusually shakes the bottle and champagne splashes out hitting the top glass, knocking it over.

Falling, the glass crumbles into splinters, each of which ends in all the other glasses below.

A few of these glasses also fall and break, generating a hell of a champagne waterfall. The pyramid of glasses manages to stand up overall, but people cannot

Angry Waiters   *Federico Fumagalli*

drink any more champagne because of the fear of splinters and fragments everywhere in the surviving glasses. It's a sticky bubbly mess.

The Maître d' looks at her as if it was her last day alive:

"And now?" he tells her, widening his arms, I guess with all the intentions to strangle her.

All other Passengers look at her too: and now? How do they drink free champagne?

We also look at her: and now? Who is going to clean up? Hopefully not the guy from Cremella.

Usually Champagne Waterfall is carried out so:

At midnight they play 'YMCA' by Village People, and the Maître d' accompanies the dreaming celebrities on the staircase, while our Dancing Team begins dancing around the bar like a drunken train.

My colleagues and I, in the meanwhile, what do we do?

When we are done with the heaviest of the services – on Thursday there is The Lobster – we gather in Bernini dining room at 23.15 where Head Waiters assign each of us a role to play. On this occasion I am the 'Champagne Tray Bringer', and my role is to walk around with a huge tray full of flutes, handing them to the thirsty Passengers.

The thing is: from 23.15 to 00.00, what do we do?
Nothing.
Really: a bloody nothing!

Angry Waiters   *Federico Fumagalli*

We stay there sitting down, waiting for the signal at midnight, and this is something that pisses us off pretty much, because most of the times, to be on duty in time, we skip our dinner.

So why can't we arrive on duty a little bit later, allowing us enough time to eat, relax, and start again? How can we relax on empty stomachs?

I'm sure that at the highest rank of the company somebody enjoys watching us knackered without stop ☺ing.

However, at 00.00, the music starts and we all come out like bats flying around our posts to play our game.

I'm fooling around with my maxi-tray full of glasses, having a good look at all the girls in miniskirts, when suddenly a couple of girls lose their balance and fall down the deck, three floors down.

What the...?!

No, no... I must be really tired; when I open my eyes again, they are still leaning on the golden balustrade, watching the show. Then, I don't know how, they both turn their heads and come towards me. Are they coming to me because I'm handsome, or because I have champagne in my hands?

Of course the reason is the champagne, and when they are close enough I have to scream to be heard over the loud music:

"Hey! How many of you?!"

"Two."

"Two of you? Wow!" I reply.

~130~

Angry Waiters   *Federico Fumagalli*

"No, dear: two glasses, please…" they answer.

But just as they are about to grab their glasses, I walk two paces backwards: I don't do that because I want to play tricks, but because suddenly the Head Waiter's words come to my mind: "Give away the champagne, make everybody happy, and try not to end up in prison!"

Here the under twenty-one are not allowed to drink alcohol. Absolutely not.

I correct myself: they can drink all the alcohol they want and get wasted and stoned and pregnant, who cares? It's us the ones who are forbidden from serving it to them.

The whole ship is surrounded by signs to remember that we can't sell or give alcohol to the under twenty-one. American law is very strict about this matter, and there are heavy sanctions behind the corner. Let's think that I give alcohol to these two girls: if they drink and nothing happens and nobody has seen me, I'm safe. But if something happens to them, like they get drunk and feel sick, and even worse somebody else has seen me – fucking witnesses – then I'm in a world of brata. Also, I would spend my youth smashing stones in a remote prison.

Since this is not my dream, I ask the two girls: "How old are you? Are you over twenty-one?"

"…yes…"

"Of course. Can I see your ID?"

"We don't have it here… we left it up in our cabin…"

Angry Waiters *Federico Fumagalli*

they blush.

"*Ma va?!*" (Sarcastic Italian for 'Oh really?!')? "Then, let's go up into your cabin...", but they roll their eyes and disappear cursing the hell out of me.

Near the library I meet a very thick crowd of people and I take the chance to thin out my tray that after a long time starts to feel heavy on my hands.

Here too there are bunches of hot girls 1.90 metres tall who look like they just came out of kindergarten, and they obviously want to drink champagne out of the feeding bottle. There's lot of people, and my glasses quickly disappear. I try not to be seen by those chicks, advancing into the crowd shouting "Excuse me! Andiamo!", but hands appear from everywhere and I don't have the time to stop all the young ladies that in half a second grab glasses with both hands and throw down their necks the content, risking to ruin my existence and my already poor bank account. For each glass swallowed I lose seven years of my miserable life. I'm sweating hard. I'm all wet.

I give a furtive look around to make sure no Head Waiters or Supervisors have seen me, I quickly drink a glass of champagne – it could be the last one of my life – then, not seeing anybody in the surroundings, I increase my speed and go back in the galley where I change my tray and I change my role without permission, writing with my pen on the schedule's task list. Now my self chosen role is to clear out the empty glasses that Passengers have left everywhere, even

Angry Waiters   *Federico Fumagalli*

inside the vases and behind plants. I grab an empty tray and walk around.

Later on I hear two Head Waiters discussing about service, and the subject is: 'Who gave the drinks to the teenagers in the library? What a f*****g idiot! If something happens…'

They spot me, I ☺ them back. I keep on walking as if nothing ever happened, and nobody will ever suspect me, unless they go to check the CCTV…

…unless they check the CCTV…

I breathe deeply.

My tray is full of dirty glasses; some are empty, some half empty, some are even full, but Passengers left them somewhere and I have to collect everything: someone might brake them causing physical damage, cuts, and complaints. Especially complaints. I live in a world of complaints.

It sometimes happens that people just take a sip from the glass and decide they don't like it, so they leave it in the most hidden places. I pick them up, and I continue doing my wrong job. And… other Passengers, seeing that I have glasses almost full, they think that those glasses are indeed clean and new, champagne still sparkling for them.

"Can I take one?" Someone asks me.

Only then I give them the best of my ☺s: "It's there for you!"

I make them happy; I don't end up in prison: I do exactly what the Head Waiter has told me. I go back to

Angry Waiters   *Federico Fumagalli*

the galley to empty the tray, grinning stupidly to the thought of giving out second-mouth champagne.

Eventually my shift finishes, and I can come back to my lovely coffin to sleep, or maybe today I can go up to the Crew Bar to have a drink and a Mars bar.

~~16~~
DAUGHTER OF THE QUEEN CAYS:
The Neverland

"Glorious day today in DOTQ Cays! We have had one of the most beautiful days of our cruise on this amazing island with a hot and sunny time! Here is your Captain speaking to you *from the bridge*! Bla bla bla… bla bla bla…"

The Captain's voice erupts from the speakers with an emphasis he wouldn't find even if he had won a Battleship, coming to the summit of it in the part "…speaking to you FROM THE BRIDGE!"

I like when he says that, but for Christ's sake: not when I am sleeping!

Oh yeah, he is really happy, positive, and he always says *Yes* (Never say No!).

His voice catches everyone's attention, not because it's interesting, but because it's played loudly through the speakers in our cabins and in every Passenger's cabin, as if we were in the communist era during the Chinese and North Korean revolution. I hear it all of a sudden, and the fright almost kills me. I am sleeping! It's 15.30 and this guy wakes me up: who do you think you are?

DOTQ Cays, as far as I am told by a useless Italian Head Waiter, is a micro-island owned by the company, on to whose soil can only walk its Passengers and

Angry Waiters   *Federico Fumagalli*

Crew. It's just like a private island, where somebody promises less than half day in paradise. Nobody actually lives on the island, except for the staff.

But… not all this is true: first of all, the name of the island is not DOTQ Cays; that's only the port of call used by the company, which is located at the southernmost tip of an island called Eleuthera, east of Nassau. The rest of this island is inhabited by real people, and there is also a small airport.

However, for Passengers and Crew there is only one way to reach it: a tender from the ship. I'm surprised that Junior Waiters are not asked to push them ashore.

When I'm on duty on the island I start at 06.30 in the Horizon Court with the Lido Breakfast shift until 09.30.

At 09.45 I proceed toward the 'Gangway Deck 4 Midship' and jump on the taxi boat. The ship is standing in the middle of the sea because there is no port for docking, and the taxi boat is the only way to reach the land. I swipe my Laminex card (the magnetic card that allows me to enter and exit the ship) into the electronic machine and I'm ready to go. At 10.00 I disembark and I can stay half an hour to get tanned, relax in a hammock, or lay down under a palm tree waiting for a coconut to land on my ugly face. At 10.30 lunch for the crew is ready under a wooden arcade.

Finally something nice!

11.00 I start my duty on the beach.

Attraction Number One for the Passengers is

Angry Waiters *Federico Fumagalli*

obviously the food that makes them crazy.

Attraction Number One for me is the ladies in bikinis.

A new service that I notice but I never do is 'Cleaning Hands', where some of my colleagues really have the displeasure of washing and disinfecting all the sweaty and greasy hands of our friendly Passengers, armed with a bottle of special liquid soap whose content doesn't need to be rinsed because is quickly absorbed by the skin. This mysterious liquid is the only weapon to fight the Battle against the Solitary Germ, which usually hides between the epidermis and blood vases of the unconscious Passenger.

But I am lucky, for once, and I'm on duty at the 'Fruit Buffet' under a big wooden hut and a temperature of one thousand degrees Celsius.

All I have to do is to replace the plastic cutlery, plastic plates and paper napkins from the buffet, without even cleaning tables because Passengers are invited to throw away their garbage themselves.

Something catches my eye; it's a sign. When I read it, I can't decide what is better: laughing, or burn the whole place down and throw coconuts at the ship and sink it.

The reason? The sign is almost the same as the one I once put on the Horizon Court buffet to teach Passengers how to use the garbage bin: here, someone used similar words to teach Passengers how to clean their tables after lunch, how and where to throw away their garbage. But... I've been told off big time when I

Angry Waiters   *Federico Fumagalli*

did it! The Head Waiter wanted to kill me! Why here has it been allowed? And by who?! Who did it?! Who stole my idea?!

Calm down. Calm down. Keep calm and replace the cutlery.

I make the most of it for staying a little while in peace, relaxing, ☺ing with pleasure and taking some pictures. I put on my sunglasses, otherwise I can't see anything under all that shining sun and I fool around and check and replace. Walking back and forth along my side, I have all the time to take care of the situation, but mostly I just look at the young ladies who are having a Tanning Competition, playing at who is tanning in the most hidden and prohibited places of their skin, lowering their bra and moving slips left and right for a total darkening, showing limbs of fresh flesh to the eye of the maniac.

Finally, I can enjoy an interesting service where nobody comes to break my balls.

I think.

And I'm wrong.

Here he comes, the Austrian F&B Manager, who is patrolling the field to make sure everything is done his way. His duty is also to get everybody to follow the hygiene rules of the USPH, even on the beach.

Now: why me?

Why, with one thousand two hundred Crew members, You, Austrian F&B, have to tell me that I am not allowed to wear sunglasses? I can't see without

Angry Waiters   *Federico Fumagalli*

them, and even the guys working on the grill are wearing them, but *there* it's OK. So, why *here* it's not? Why in *my* area sunglasses are not allowed, and somewhere else are? Why aren't my glasses conforming to hygiene rules?

OK, I put them back in my pocket. Just… go away.

But do you bet that as soon as you turn the corner, I put them back on my ugly face again, and then you will have to come back?

I'll have you run a marathon back and forth just for my sunglasses, you mentally retarded.

At 14.00 I go away from this island that is nothing but a stretch of beach full of rocks where there is nothing, not even ice cream. The part of the real island has been sealed off and concealed to the eyes of the Passengers to make them believe that this is truly an uninhabited island.

And then, if I have to be awaken by the Captain while I am trying to recover before another shift, it's logic that I go on duty in the dining room with a killer mood.

~~17~~
WAR OF THE WORLDS

These days there is still an ongoing war between the USA and Iraq. It's commonly known that America is a *pro-peace* nation: this is demonstrated by the fact that it's full of tireless superheroes that fight for freedom and peace; it is showed by the fact that firearms are allowed in almost every household; the US army has been present in almost every conflict fought in history since the day of creation.

Unfortunately, superheroes began to mind their own business remaining inside their comics' pages: why risk their life in a useless country like Afghanistan? What's in there for them?

Captain Bush is not really having a great time, trying to sort it out with halal chocolates and sweet talks. Not even his God is helping him, reason why all of a sudden assault rifles, bombs and drones are deployed.

Passengers are nervous, and for this reason we are forbidden off any comment, because our opinions not only aren't required, not only are useless, but they would surely lead to a complaint and the total erasure of our tips.

I must carry on ☺ing and pretending not to know anything of what's going on (War? Where?!) just to avoid misunderstandings. At the same time I look like a careless ignorant, because Passengers, being Americans, want that *we* worry about the same things

Angry Waiters Federico Fumagalli

that *they* are worried about. It's a very messy situation to handle, and I'm not sure how to behave. Also, things get more complicated on the night of 'French Dinner'.

Usually, for the French Dinner we put French flags on the tables; the menu is in French with English translation; I am also disguised in French dress, with red-white-blue bow tie and striped belt.

A couple with a political look, sitting at my station, ask me:

"Excuse me, Alfredo..." and the discussion takes already a bad turn, because my name is Federico, "...are you sure we are having a French Dinner tonight?"

"Yes, of course!" I reply promptly, and a red alert in my brain sparks up. Something is wrong with these two rumentas.

"Oh... because you know... usually there are flags on the table... Why are they missing? Did you forget them or what?"

'Did you want to eat them?' I think.

There you go, the husband has been on a cruise many times and he knows better than me about flags and bullshit. Now, how do I explain to him that we didn't put French flags because France refused to help USA in the Iraq war and we just wanted to avoid hurting their pacifist feelings?

Simple, I don't explain.

The Real Professional Waiter always lies, I've been taught at school by a very old and expert Maître d', so

Angry Waiters   *Federico Fumagalli*

I invent the stupidest excuse on Earth: "No, no… it's just that the company is making new flags… the previous set was old and gone… Soon we will have New Shiny French Flags! You want me to send you one at home?" and I ☺.

But the man doesn't take it. "Alfredo, is it because of the war? Coward French?"

"Fe-de-ri-co." I say. *'Now I paint a French flag on your forehead'*.

Well done! The man isn't so stupid after all, and he got it straight away. Also he gives a nice 'Coward' to the French People.

Help.

My Waiter is in the kitchen, my eyes are scanning around to find a Head Waiter to give me a hand – mission impossible – so I decide to tell the couple that "Yes, it's because of the war". Besides, the couple are not fools, and I also apologise for the lie (on the other hand, waiters have to lie; never trust a waiter's word, trust me). At the end of the discussion, I come out pretty well, though the man keeps calling me 'Alfredo'. Alfredo is the name of our Fettuccine pasta (noodles pasta) that we find in the 'Always Available' section of the kitchen.

The first time that I have to face this section is like taking part in a difficult birth: my Waiter orders me to go and collect a grilled salmon, which I don't know where to take.

"It's in the *Always available* section!" He explains to

Angry Waiters   *Federico Fumagalli*

me with a very questionable pronunciation.

What reaches my ears is also questionable, so I don't understand it. I pretend I have understood and I enter the kitchen with a questionable look on my face, and I ask around *where is* and *what is* this *Always Available*. Two words I have never heard before, and therefore I don't know how to pronounce.

"Excuse me, where is the Auleys Auei...vebol? Oulueis Avueila... Aueilavol?"

"What?!"

"Where is the Auauays... Aua... Avua... Aueuebol?"

"Fucking Italian, get lost!"

Then I ask the gigantic black chef (which, for an unfortunate coincidence is working exactly at the station I am looking for, just that I did not realise it, and there are no flashing flags on the ceiling with the arrow pointing down to announce that *THE ALWAYS AVAILABLE ARE HERE IN FRONT OF YOUR NOSE)*:

"Excuse me, I'm looking for the Aluays Auevebol...? Aouluais Ave... Aue... Aueueuevebol?"

"...The fuck you saying?!"

"Where is the section with the salmon, fettuccine... Olueis Ave... Aulueis Auvue... Auauaulueis Aueueuevabeil...?"

The now angry chef looks at me while his monumental pectorals tear away his uniform:

"You taking the piss? Get da fuck outta here! I'll smash your face!"

Angry Waiters   *Federico Fumagalli*

Ignorance... not something to be proud of.

While this couple at the table are monopolising the pain to my scrotum, I see my Waiter coming back to the station with nothing in his hands (one of the big No-nos, on a cruise ship, is coming in and out from the galley with empty hands).

The couple clearly want to carry on conversating, for which I have no time.

"Alfredo, by the way, where are you from?"

It's written on my badge that: "I'm from Italy."

"Ah, nice! *Como estas?*"

"No no no: you people deserve the all hurricanes that hit you every year!" and I run away to the other side leaving my Waiter alone with the anti-French couple. I'm sure they would ask him the same question they asked me, and I don't want to be there listening to the same shameful answer.

The very bad thing about the war is that we risk staying here in the Caribbean rather than cruising in the Mediterranean. We are all looking forward to go to Europe, because the cruise will be less stressful and the places more interesting.

The Crew's mood is thundering, with strong winds of rebellion and dark clouds of incoming damage. Many of us are ready to resign in case we stayed in the Caribbean, and I am one of them.

Still because of the war in Iraq, many Passengers begin cancelling their bookings in the Mediterranean,

Angry Waiters   *Federico Fumagalli*

and the risk of staying here is growing higher: if there are no Cruising Passengers, there are no Cruising Tips for the Crew, and who the hell wants to work all day in change of less money than now? Even the Atlantic Cruise is almost empty, and that means twelve days of mental sickness where Passengers would start to complain about everything, even about the good weather, and I can't blame them because for twelve days they – we all – have to stay on board this floating city without walking on solid ground. We all would become nervous. You would cut the tension with a knife.

But after a few days there are new rumours running through the escape doors: we will all go to Europe anyway, and the news gets confirmed when Mr Bush declares to have won a war by bombing a country with chocolate eggs and get-well-soon cards.

Now that everything is fixed and the ideas are clear we are happy and tired, but suddenly there's a new meeting where someone in charge appears with a pair of giant scissors to announce the *Cutting of the Staff*.

Though we'll cruise in Europe anyway, the ship will remain almost empty with only one third of Tipping Passengers; for this reason the company can't guarantee the same money to everybody. The only solution is to cut the number of Working Slaves, maybe by sending them on holiday for a few months until there will be a full ship again.

Only among the waiting staff, around fifty are to be

Angry Waiters   *Federico Fumagalli*

discarded, probably without any criteria, because decisions will be made in an office somewhere in America, and they can't be changed or discussed.

My always alert ears grab a signal which says: 'We accept volunteers for disembarkation!' and the antenna rises up in an instant. I make mental note of this and mark the point of my situation; I evaluate pros and cons; I'm 22 and I'm not living; I want to work around the world and *see* it, so until I stay trapped in here, I will never make it. I want to get the hell out of here!

Nobody believes me when I say so (because being Italian brings too many advantages to refuse them), but unfortunately I'm not up for it, and one day later I enter the Maître d' office to volunteer my disembarkation.

Multiple are the reasons, and they will come out very soon.

And what I said until now is not even enough to give up so soon. Until now is nothing.

What really deserves my farewell is the Top of all services, the hell of all hells, the tiredness of all tirednesses, the pain in the arse of all pains in all arses:

~~18~~

THE ~~DYING~~ DINING ROOM SHIFT: wHELLcome...

The ~~Dying~~ Dining Room shift lasts for two weeks and it's the hardest and heaviest. It wouldn't be hard and heavy if it wasn't for thousands of Bosses to stress us up and put everyone under pressure.

It is also subdivided in three basic shifts to which we have to add other small duties, extra services, micro-tasks.

We start early with Breakfast, proceeding with Lunch and ending with Dinner... all in the Dining Rooms. We can forget the Horizon Court and the easy life of the buffet.

Among these three basic columns of the day, hidden between one minute and another, there are other 'Optional Services' that I can either choose to do, or not. Usually, I choose *not*. If I don't do them, I have to pay somebody else to work for me, and it always happens for the Teatime and the Wine Tasting services.

The Turnaround day – circle of new shifts – starts on Saturday night, but since the morning I can spot the first disagreement: indeed it's better for me to go and check on the noticeboard to make sure that my supposed time off in Fort Lauderdale has truly been voided.

Angry Waiters   *Federico Fumagalli*

On Saturday morning I get up at 04.45 because Passengers have to disembark.

My happiness is limited due to the early shift, because usually I could finish at 09.30 and be free until 16.00. I could fool around in the town, I could go to the beach, maybe to Miami; I could do whatever I feel like.

I go down to the Crew Mess for a quick breakfast and subsequently I check the noticeboard to see where I should work in the evening, in which dining room, at which station…

Problem: the more I look at the shift, the more I am disappointed. There's something wrong: written small and disguised between the other names I can read 'Frederico Fumagayli, Embarkation Team 11.00 to 14.00 with white gloves and green uniform'.

The problem is not my name and surname spelled wrongly again, but my ex-free time: no more of it. I now have three extra working hours, and I don't ☺ at all.

Also, Embarkation Team is the worst shift: there are two of them, and the second one is from 14.00 to 16.00.

My patience has gone, with this shift I can't even go out, so I decide to go back to my cabin and take a nap before starting smiling endlessly.

At one minute to 11.00 I should be already at the meeting, but at 11.20 Marco worryingly wakes me up knocking at the door. No, maybe he is not knocking it, he's trying to burst inside and drag me to the

~148~

Angry Waiters   *Federico Fumagalli*

Supervisor.

"Federico! Porca Madonna! You are late!" he yells.

Fuck! I still have to dress up!

I reach my position at Deck 5 where new Passengers will enter the ship, but I realise that I forgot my white gloves, so I run like a hunted rabbit back to my cabin looking for the pair of bloody white gloves which are: one in the bag among other white things, and the other one… I can't find the other one.

Bastard!

Wearing the left-hand glove I'm still looking for the right-hand one, I open my drawers and… there you go! Found it!

I exit the door quickly trying to wear the right-hand glove… but… it doesn't fit my hand…

…because is another left-hand glove. Damn the day when I decided it was a good idea to have two pairs of gloves!

I re-enter my cabin, throwing everything around and I find a right-hand glove under the bag of my Polish room-mate, a little bit too big for me because he has hands the size of Gulliver's, but I keep it anyway and running faster than light I reappear on duty where luckily there is no Head Waiter waiting to give me a warning. The Supervisor disappeared.

Then I realise that...

'Fuck!'

I'm in the wrong place!

When I find the right place, my *friendly* Austrian

Angry Waiters   *Federico Fumagalli*

F&B is there waiting for me, arms wide open and a big dangerous smile, as if to say 'This time I forgive you, but next time... down in doggy style!'

From now on I enter the Kingdom of Boredom: to each one of us the Head Waiter has previously assigned one placement, where we have to stand waiting for the new Passengers to come in.

My position is at the end of the Art Gallery and each time new Passengers come close to me I simply have to direct them toward the lifts, where they will find other Crew Members available to take them to their respective decks and rooms.

Clear and simple.

I'm standing there nice and quiet telling everybody: "Good afternoon! On this way!" showing the direction with my hand and index finger, when I realise that my eyelids slowly slowly are closing down without mercy, and my stomach claims lunch.

Luckily for me Anchana comes to tell me that it's my turn for my twenty minute break, and she will replace me whilst I go to the Crew Mess where obviously there is a never-ending queue for the feeding trough (the buffet), and the watering trough (the drinks machine) is forever out of service. Swallowing what the Chef calls Food for Humans, I think of my duty which I reckon to be useless. There are thousands of signs and twenty colleagues to indicate the way to the lifts, and where I am there is enough visibility to see either the ones before or after me. I'm convinced more and more

Angry Waiters   *Federico Fumagalli*

that they put me on duty just for torture. I also think that Passengers are *not* idiots, so they don't really need our help.

But as soon as I set foot back in my position I change idea: why is that whole host of people wearing winter clothes? And why are they all scattering for every cardinal point? Why, if I say 'On *this* way!' they go 'The *other* way'?

I don't understand why if I tell them to go to the right, they go to the left. What is it, a challenge?

I raise my voice and shout "Ladies and gentlemen! On this way for the lifts! Andiamo!"

I feel like a traffic warden.

Even the girl ambushed at the lifts comes to give me a hand, due to an overflowing amount of newcomers that block the way. I feel like I am in an artery obstructed by cholesterol, where I play the cholesterol.

When they realise that I exist and I am there to help them, I become a Godsend from the Heavens and they submerge me with requests like "Where is my cabin? Where do I have to go? Where is the snack bar?" and they show me their Cruise Card with respective cabin number and deck letter.

I repeat that they should reach the lifts, where they will find other Crew Members available to help them (Maybe. But I had to get rid of them). The thing is that they don't listen to me.

"Where is cabin 373?" one of them asks me again.

"Madame, it depends on which deck your cabin is

Angry Waiters   *Federico Fumagalli*

located. Check the letter before the number on your Cruise Card, please." I say gently.

"Well, here it is says 'C 373'."

"Very good!" I breathe. "You have to take the lifts! Right there!" and I point my arm, my hand, my finger and my nail. She can't miss it.

But she still doesn't get it. "And once there, where?"

"Ma porca puttana!" I swear, "Go to the lifts! Somebody will guide you!" (maybe) and my patience is digging six feet under. I'm getting irritated and pissed off, and it's not good. I must ☺ and be kind!

At this stage I don't have the time to finish the phrase that the people behind her begin yelling where they could find their cabins, and I get filled up with questions to which I don't know the answers. The only answer is "On this way! On this way to the lifts! Andiamo!" but the queue is getting longer... and even the Crew at the lifts are shouting at me because I'm blocking the flow of two thousand eight hundred Passengers. I'm going to be in big brata because nobody listens to me, creating such a crazy mess where somebody tells me "Aloha!" referring to the deck's name, and I reply "Hello!" thinking that I got a kind of greeting, and giving the impression of me being a real retarded.

To get me out of brata (the girl who came few minutes earlier to help me has simply disappeared; probably she jumped at sea wearing a life jacket made of stone) the Supervisor sends me another couple of

~152~

Angry Waiters Federico Fumagalli

girls. The queue has reached a length that the Company has never seen before, and that is just because nobody pays attention to me; everybody is standing by me, waiting for answers even before I get the questions. When the two girls come to me, they grab random Passengers dragging them in the lifts without mercy. I think my colleagues are cursing at me: for my fault they are all missing their lunch break. The chaos at my station is just too much, and we need all the available staff to sort it out.

Eventually we make it, and though I better run and hide away from my colleagues (they are planning to kill me one by one, but I still have this feeling that soon I will die sinking). Even so I can't hide a grin of sadist satisfaction: I had lunch and they hadn't; I'm not really sorry for them, and this makes me ☺☺☺ a lot: how many times did I miss my lunch because of them?

Sweet revenge…

After two and a half hours I said 'On this way!' to at least one thousand six hundred Passengers, and the monotony grows, so much that it becomes automatic for me to announce 'Good afternoon! On this way!' and indicate direction with my arm, destination lifts.

It's so automatic and I am so bored that I answer the same thing even to the guy who asks me where the toilets are, and to the two fat ladies who want to know where the Casino is. I can't stand it any more, I must wait until 14.00 to finish my shift, and if I want to go out I need to wait for the opening of the Time Windows

Angry Waiters   *Federico Fumagalli*

at 14.30, allowing me only one hour of freedom. This bullshit of the Time Windows makes everybody nuts, either for entering or exiting the ship.

At the end of it all, I made my great impression to the new Passengers, and I have the time to do the only thing that's left to do: sleeping.

At 16.00, I wake up again to change uniform and be on duty at 16.29 in the new dining room, at the new station, where of course fifty per cent of items are missing: glasses, cups, breadbaskets, bread plates, bread knives, water jugs...

'Ladies and gentlemen! There you go, welcome to the new Passengers! Uglier and hungrier than ever! Open your arms wide open to the new wave of Rumentas and Cippettones who will give us harder times for this new exciting cruise! YO HO HO OO!'

Angry Waiters   *Federico Fumagalli*

~~19~~
BREAKFAST IN HELL

06.15: My G-Shock alarm rings for twenty seconds, then I feel my vibrator (I mean: the vibrations coming from my phone), which I always put in some difficult place to find, so that I'm forced to get up and find it, stop it, or break it. I wear the wrong uniform, I wash my face, switch the light on, put gel on my hair, I run out of the door, shave my face, I put on the correct uniform (all those things not necessarily in that order), and I go to consume my breakfast.

At 07.00, I'm in position in Donatello dining room for the roll call. While the Waiters prepare their mise en place for the tables, I as a Junior Waiter have to look on the noticeboard and check what kind of cleaning I've been assigned to finish before 07.30. There are heaps of things to do with different tasks, either in Donatello or Bernini. For example, I could be 'Cleaning Doors', where I must wipe one of the two rotating doors and make them shine; I could be 'Cleaning Floor', mopping all the marble stripes that run on the floor like a disorienting labyrinth; I could be 'Cleaning Wood', in this case, armed with blue towel and chlorine I must pass all over the handrails; I could be 'Cleaning Glasses', to clean windows and mirrors in the whole dining room; I could be doing 'Linen clothes in Bernini', to put tablecloths on the thousand tables in that dining room; I could be 'Checking Girls',

Angry Waiters　　　　　　　　　*Federico Fumagalli*

where I get hold of the half asleep ladies and I give them a shining and cheerful mood, ready to work with a big, big ☺, but unfortunately this task always happens to *the others*.

At 07.30, after I did my job, I can finally start to work at my station. In the morning I work with somebody different from the evening, but he/she is the same for lunch.

If it's Sunday, is a bad thing. It's bad because the night before we had to put the clock 'one hour forward' and Passengers come later than usual. Before 08.30 usually nobody arrives, and then, at 09.15 they all come together and we all get pissed off because the doors close at 09.30 and we know we will never finish. We risk missing our break because on Sunday morning we have to get in the kilometric queue to collect our ridiculous salary and at 11.30 we must be in the dining room again for lunch shift.

I don't really want to explain the breakfast shift, but for the benefit of knowledge I'll do it anyway.

First of all, I must keep in mind that this breakfast has been thought by our bosses for Passengers belonging to the category M.A., and what do M.A want? Eating a lot, for free, arriving late and pretending to finish ASAP.

The menu presents various items, from cold food to hot food, and since there is no buffet (*'We kindly invite the Passengers who request the buffet to move their asses and go to the Horizon Court. Have an Excellent*

~156~

Angry Waiters   *Federico Fumagalli*

day, you all!') I must go and collect everything in the galley. The Passenger is not allowed to get up from their seat and look for something, this is a strong policy: there must be someone (a Waiter, a Head Waiter, a Supervisor, a Junior Waiter, a jellyfish) always present in the area nearby to serve him with a smile on his face. The Passengers are on holiday, they do not have to get up and sit down continuously, and we are there for them.

If my Waiter doesn't help me, I must unravel between eight fruit juices, fresh fruit, dried prunes, cantaloupe and honeydew melon, Fruit of the Day which is always something tropical, yoghurt, milk, cereals (cold, warm, hot, burning). Obviously before beginning duty it's better to read the menu carefully, especially for me. It's better also to ask questions about what is not known: there are lot of things that I don't know and I *absolutely* want to avoid giving the impression of me being an incompetent.

The first time happens after just ten minutes due to my ignorance toward the meaning of the word 'wedges', but just because I don't want to show that I don't know how to carry out such a simple task, I prefer to carry on as nothing is going to happen. A task is always simple *if* you know it. The thing is, I have no idea what these *wedges* are.

Apple wedges, as everyone else knows, are just simple slices of this bloody fruit, served in a silver cup and sprinkled with cinnamon, and they are prepared in

~157~

the kitchen. Very, very simple.

My Waiter takes the order, writing on his docket 'apple wedges'. I think *What the hell are these wedges...*', then he sees me still at the station, so he shouts at me to move: "Can you manage it?", "Of course!" I reply, and I run in the galley, wondering and pondering.

After thinking for five infinite minutes, I come to the conclusion that 'wedges' must be the English brand of some of those apples that I never met before. I don't even ask around, avoiding looking like a fool, just to test my intelligence.

I go to the Fruit Station and I check the little stamps on at least fifteen to eighteen apples, but not even one of them has the name: *Wedges*. I ask to the Thai chef behind the counter, a few metres away, *if* and *where* I can have some of those 'Fucking Apple Wedges', and straight away he indicates to me the correct counter using his arm, hand and index finger.

I don't trust him, I have just been on that counter to check eighteen apples, and I am convinced that what I'm doing is right (I'm not dumb, am I?). Also, on the shelf over the counter, from where I am, I can spot heaps of silver cups, but not apples. I pretend I understood what he said, so I take a plate and I collect two of those whole apples, a red one and a green one so that the Passengers could also choose the colour: Yeah! Do the job properly! That's the way!

I enter triumphant to my station, big ☺ on my face,

but my Waiter doesn't have the time to send me to hell because not only he is in big brata up to his neck (the station is totally full and I have been away an eternity), but now he also has to cut and peel my apples without touching them with his hands. He can only use knife and fork and lot of ability, which I think he doesn't have: as per USPH rules, *never* touch food with hands, especially in front of Passengers. I can see from his facial expression that he is thinking about how he could possibly kill me, later on. This task of slicing and cutting fruit in front of the guests without physical contact is something that I learnt at school many years ago, but *nobody* does it any more and anywhere in the world for the simple reason that it takes you way *too much time*. And on a cruise ship, the last thing you want is to waste time.

My Waiter is about to explode when one of the apples slips away from his knife's grip, falling and rolling on the ground. At that exact moment I run away in the galley, trying hard not to laugh at his face.

The first day of Breakfast for me is terrifying, though the following won't be much better. The Dining Room shift which includes Breakfast lasts for two weeks, and as soon as I learn how to carry out a decent service with limited mistakes, they send me to Horizon Court again, and I forget everything.

Moreover, the fact that I can't trust anyone increases the risk of mistakes; cooperation between colleagues doesn't exist, and each error is equal to an extra trip in

Angry Waiters   *Federico Fumagalli*

or out of the galley or a trip with more items on a tray.

I should always exit the galley with food on my big wooden tray, and the more the food, the less the trips.

We all have to make sure that we are carrying the proper food but, more importantly: we have to make sure that we are carrying *our* food, making sure it's not *someone* else's food.

The habit, among the little lazy bastards who work with me, is to steal the dishes that I have already placed on my tray. It's already annoying when it's material items, but when it comes to see your own food going away with somebody else, well… this makes me even angrier.

It happens for example that I have to fight with Julia, a very short Rumanian (no more than one metre and a dick tall) who, since she can't reach the plastic covers on top of the counters, she decides that is more convenient to take the covers from my plates and transfer them onto her plates, while I am running around like a headless chicken asking *where are* and *what are* the 'Sunny side up eggs'. In that way, my '*Fucked up* eggs' get cold.

As soon as I realise what she's doing I kindly scream to her to "Put everything back *now*!" but she doesn't care and she sweetly replies me something that I will learn later on and that you could pronounce like "Duden pizta muotti!" which means 'Go back in to your mother's pussy!', so she is inviting me to go back to where I came from. Then, with all my knowledge of

Angry Waiters   *Federico Fumagalli*

Rumanian I surprise her by calmly telling her 'Sugi pula!' which is a not-very-polite form of 'Give me a blowjob!'

I learn 'sugi pula' thanks to my Rumanian colleagues: when we are in the galley waiting for the lemon-butter-cheese in Canaletto shift, we are all in line. It's about forty of us. We wait for the pastry chefs to come up from Bernini with their big trolley containing bread, and when they walk in front of us we are all silent. Only when the first in line raises his arm we all fill our lungs with air and scream all together the most chaotic of all "SUGI PULAAAAAAAA!!!!!!".

I come back to my station late, hopefully still carrying *my* stuff, and I put the tray on the Clean Area. My waiter quickly throws down plates to the already complaining Passengers, claiming food with mouth wide open like newborn birds. If he doesn't need my help, I take the other orders, I collect the dirty tray and I rocket in the galley. I throw the tray to the Indian dishwashers, I take a new one and I go to fill it.

So: pancakes, first row on the left; cheese omelettes at the end. Cold stuff: yoghurt, salmon, fruit juice: grapefruit, pineapple, prunes and apple. Then I need toast: a bagel for the salmon, one brown toast, one English muffin, and... But... No... I forgot...

Damn! I forgot to bring with me the breadbasket!

Toast must be carried *only* and *exclusively* inside the breadbasket with its napkin. No other way.

What if I use another plate or a bowl that I can cover?

Angry Waiters   *Federico Fumagalli*

No, no, no: the guy on duty at the toast machine would refuse even to put bread inside the toaster if I don't show him first that I am equipped with a breadbasket conforming to the 'Three S' rule: Spotless, Shining, *Stolen*.

Still the problem remains: I don't have one with me and I can't steal any, because there are not any in sight.

I must take the risk: I leave the tray there and I run to my station to collect the basket, but my Waiter spots me and becomes as upset as a hyena: first because I came out without food, second because I forgot the breadbasket, third because if I arrived with the food I would not have had my toast anyway, fourth because I'm wasting time, fifth because he is a dickhead.

I return to the kitchen with my basket, Toast Man makes my toast, but from my tray the salmon and two juices have vanished.

"Porca Madonna! Who did that?!" I ask gently to Toast Man.

"I don't know."

Of course he knows, but rule number one is 'Don't trust anyone, especially Toast Men'.

I quickly explain to him what kind of contraception his mother should have used with her customers and I get hold once more of the missing items, I exit the galley placing the tray in the Clean Area. For the pancake I have to go somewhere to look for its special syrup, Maple Syrup. While I'm looking for this small bottle I hear my Waiter calling me: "Fredico! The

Angry Waiters *Federico Fumagalli*

omelette wasn't with cheese! It was with mushrooms! Go and change it!"

"When I come back I break your nose!" I reply without care. "And I'm not Fredico!"

Now I need to change omelette because this time the mistake was his: he wrote me the wrong symbols. We never write the entire omelette's name, we use symbols. If on the docket I read 'CH', the omelette is cheese; if I read 'M', is mushrooms; 'H' is ham; 'T' stands for tomatoes; 'HC' is ham and cheese; HOMCHTPA is ham-onions-mushrooms-cheese-tomatoes-panda.

Maybe.

What the hell!

I return with my stuff, I refill cups with coffee, regular and decaf, I clean tables, swear, wash, dry, ☺, polish, run, fight, steal, scream, slash, crash and burn.

Until 10.00am.

~~20~~
LUNCH

After breakfast I go back to the Crew Mess for another breakfast (mine) because I'm starving, I throw down something in to my stomach and I return in my tiny doghouse for a short nap.

11.29 I rush to attack Donatello dining room and I do exactly all the things I do for dinner shift: mise en place, prepare my station, attend the meeting, listen to the news (☺, push for the wine, never say no, and from today: 'Cups on the table!! Cups on the taaable!!') then at 12.00 we all charge a battle against hunger.

Luckily lunch is rarely very busy, there is not the same amount of people than at dinner time because most of them are up in the Horizon Court, or they are tanning on the local island.

The menu changes daily, so I have to check around the galley from *where* comes out *what*, except for the line of 'Always Available' food, where the chef's specialties are always there: salmon, fettuccine Alfredo, sirloin steaks, hate.

I spend my last period of Lunch shift with the Rumanian Gabriela, girlfriend of a Slovakian friend who speaks Italian very well. I get along with her pretty well, and also our job together goes well too, which is strange for the fact that nobody wants to work with her. I don't understand why: though she is a Rumanian Waitress, she is very skilful. She doesn't get

Angry Waiters *Federico Fumagalli*

upset when she asks me for some empty 'cereal bowls', and by my misunderstanding I come back with some kind of unknown broth that doesn't even exist on the menu. She stands impassive also when she requires me to bring her some 'Meatball soup', and I come back with a dessert randomly taken from the pastry.

If I have been good, she herself prepares me a mega ice cream with caramel sauce. Instead, if I have made cock-ups like entering the galley with an order for six salads to dress with six different dressings (there are more than ten, and I have to do it myself), and exiting the galley forgetting which salad I dressed with which sauce, then I have to make the ice cream with my own hands.

Lately, we have on board the number one of all Head Waiters, Abelardo, an Italian man who works and cares for everyone, always ready to give you a hand. Probably the only one of his species, he also has quite an interesting sense of humour. All the staff are happy to work when he is on duty, even the engineers.

Sometimes, like today, he comes up with some table performance to give us a break from the abnormally boring routine of service.

I finish serving a table and I hear him calling me (correctly):

"Federico, try to get free in a couple of minutes, *we* need you!"

"*We*... Who?"

Angry Waiters   *Federico Fumagalli*

"Me!"

"Oh... OK... And what for?"

"Can you sing?"

"No. I'm the reason why deaf people don't want their hearing back."

"Perfect! Clear your throat then, I need your *special ability* to sing Happy Birthday at a table."

Great.

Singing happy birthday to Passengers isn't exactly what servers like to do.

Two minutes later I see Abelardo coming out the Galley with a cake stuffed with candles and eight waiters.

I mean: the eight waiters are simply following Abelardo; they are not actually *on* cake stuffing it with the candles.

"Come on Federico! Join the train!"

We reach a table where a family of four is eating. All other Passengers are staring at us, waiting for the show.

Abelardo signal us with his hand like an orchestra's director to start all together:

"Happy birthday to youuuuu... Happy birthday to youuuuu... Happy birthday to..."

Stop.

Abelardo asks the stunned mother:

"Excuse me, what's your name?"

"Christine, but today is not my birthd..."

Abelardo's hand waves furiously at us:

"...CHRISTIIIINE.!!!   Happy   birthday   to

~166~

Angry Waiters   *Federico Fumagalli*

youuuuuu!!!"

The lady blushes while every Passenger in the dining room claps their hands.

When silence is back and she has stopped laughing she says: "Thank you, but today is not my birthday!"

Abelardo pretends to be surprised while the rest of the family is still laughing. He looks at us in fake disbelief: "Oh my god! It's the wrong Christine! How foolish of me!"

Still holding the cake he turns around looking at other tables:

"Is there any other Christine around?"

Total silence. Nobody replies.

He then points at an old lady four tables away, eating by herself:

"You! I found you! Stay where you are! We are coming!"

We all move quickly following Abelardo until he slams the cake on the old lady's table.

In disbelief, she begins to laugh. "What are you doing?! It's not my birthday! And I'm not Christine!"

Abelardo, not giving a damn about her statements, forces her to blow the candles together with him.

"Don't lie to me! Your nose will get longer! Come on, blow with me, I want to finish and go to sleep!"

"If you insist..." She is still laughing. "But it's not my birthday..."

She blows, and Abelardo signal to us again:

"Happy birthday to youuuuu, happy birthday to

youuuu, happy birthday to..."

Stop again.

"Pardon me, so what's your name then?" he asks her.

"Stephanie! My name is Stepha..."

New signal for all of us:

"CHRISTIIIINE!!! Happy birthday to youuuuuu!"

Everyone on board applauding hard.

The old lady is almost in tears from laughter, red faced.

"But I said 'Stephanie'!"

"Well, it's not even your birthday, but enjoy the cake and have a wonderful day, eh?"

He leaves the cake on the table, he cuts it, and then after telling us to get the hell out of here, he calls to other Passengers to come join *lonely Stephanie* to sit and eat with her. He takes some extra chairs and the lady is a happy bunny surrounded by new friends.

In this Lunch shift I sometimes have some luxury time to chat with my colleagues, and I take advantage of this to learn a little bit of Polish language; I always keep in my pocket a small notebook, and every day I fill it up a bit.

If I don't take any Caramella (last minute tables for the guy from Cremella), at 14.30 I finish and I can consume the food that I've smartly stolen from the kitchen, then I return to my cage.

Evening time: same story, same place, same time, same brata.

16.29 ready in any of the dining rooms.

Depending on the days I need to wear a different uniform, but the worst is Thursday because we have to face the Monster of the Seven Seas:

~~21~~

THE LOBSTER: Gala dinner
(The Battle for the Lobster and related survival skills)

The Nightmare.

Whatever happened during the week, it can't stand in comparison with the 'Lobster Night'.

Silent night, lobster night… This is what Passengers are waiting for with greed: the Lobster.

Forget about Baked Alaska.

Forget about Champagne Waterfall.

Forget about Sex.

There's the Lobster.

During the usual meeting the Head Waiters insist more and more about the Wine Revenue story: 'Tonight's Lobster Night! Push for the wine! Push as much as you can! A glass of champagne! A cocktail! Whatever! Try to *squeeze* the Passengers! After dinner remember the Champagne Waterfall! And now… Sing and Dance!'

Oh, right… how nice. After the gala there's the Champagne Waterfall, where women will rip each other's hair fighting like wrestlers just to manage to climb to the top of the pyramid of glasses and gush out the cheapest of all sparkling wines all surrounded by camera flashes.

Lately the revenue income is not really what they

Angry Waiters   *Federico Fumagalli*

expected to be, it's too low, the drink sales are scarce and so we have to push for alcohol. What can we do if Passengers are stingy and feel like drinking iced tea?

There is the lobster, OK, and our task is to find a way to force them to drink wine, champagne, or whatever contains alcohol. The mission is to get them drunk, for the Revenue's Sake. But what if they want a Diet Coke? Do we slap them with a salmon? Let alone the fact that some of them drink hot chocolate, but this is something that I would personally do too! So why do we have to insist at *every single course?* Then we risk getting a complaint because we tried to make them all drunk.

In addition, we must increase our running skills, because for this occasion almost everybody comes down to the dining rooms rather than dining up on the self-service buffet. The high number of reservations forces us to keep quick marching rhythms until the end. This is one of the nights where *everything must go* smoothly and perfectly. *No* errors, *No* mistakes, *No* misunderstandings are allowed during Lobster Night, and we are very aware of this.

Don't forget that in competition with Ms Lobster there is the mouth-watering Mr Eye Fillet.

After the food chain to which the Passenger self attends, I arrive in the dining room faster than ever before, Lobster on my tray, heart pumping big time. My Waiter is waiting for me, already brandishing fork and knife, he throws down the scorching plates on the

Angry Waiters   Federico Fumagalli

table, and then I pass him a side plate. This way, he has to separate the meat from the carapace directly on the plate of the Passenger, in front of them, and then I pass around the table pouring the sauce with a spoon trying not to fall in the temptation of smearing their stylish gala dresses.

And up to here, it would be easy, if I may say so.

However, since a few days ago there's been a change, the news of the Gala Dinner made some of us laugh, some of us pissed off.

As someone has been caught stealing Lobsters for personal purposes (nutritional purposes, I hope), and Lobsters cost a lot of money, from this moment if we want to order Lobster in the galley we need to go there holding a special docket made by our Waiter inclusive of the number of Lobsters required, plus of course the regular docket for the rest of the food. The separate docket indicating the Lobsters is not enough by itself: we Junior Slaves must run around looking for any available Head Waiter to *sign* it.

And what does it take?

It takes time!

And what is it that I don't have?

Time!

I have to turn my head left and right, jumping up and down in the hope of spotting one Head Waiter with a pen (sometimes they don't have one, hence my habit of having at least five with me: one for me, one for the

~172~

Angry Waiters   *Federico Fumagalli*

Head Waiter, one for the Passenger, one for the colleague who lost his, and one to stab the foreskin of my dear work*mates*).

And to the Head Waiter, of course, I have to arrive with empty hands, because I can't walk around the dining room holding a tray full of dirty plates. Only *after* I have made the Head Waiter sign the docket, I can *return* to the rendezvous station to collect the tray and go to the kitchen passing through Start without collecting the twenty dollars.

By calamity I find Mr Martin, the largest Head Waiter on board, his belly almost coming out of his shirt, I hand him my docket and I kindly ask if he can sign it for two Lobsters. My pen magically appears in my hands, pointing at him: there is no time to waste!

"This docket is not good!" he yells at me. "You need the *white one!*"

Mine is light blue, but what's the difference? The main thing is that at the end of the night the Lobsters signed on the dockets match with the Lobsters sold.

I go back to my Waiter, asking him to write the order on a *white* docket.

"You still here?! Where's the bloody food?!" he yells at me, too.

"Sorry, but Fat Martin doesn't want to sign it because it's light blue. He wants a white one." I reply.

"What a fat asshole! Here you go, your white docket! And move your ass! We got more Passengers! Bread is missing! Refill water jugs! Ask for the drinks! Go!

Angry Waiters   *Federico Fumagalli*

Go! Go!" he says, waving his hand.

I come back to Fat Martin:

"You see how white is this docket? It's shining! Will you sign it, please?".

But I feel something wrong. His nostrils are enlarging, oxygen filling up his lungs. His belly is expanding like a balloon.

'Is that a baby?' I'm tempted to ask. *'When did you eat him?'*

"What's this, huh?! Toilet paper?! You need the white docket from the docket pad with the stripes on it! Not any white flying paper! Wake up little boy!" he yells at me. Everyone seems to be yelling at me without consideration.

His breath stinks of red wine.

"Why? Isn't this the same? It's white as you told me!"

"Don't talk back to me! How you dare?! When I tell you something, just do it!"

"Yeah, yeah, yeah…" I murmur.

I run back to my station, pissed off like a cayman, expecting to be insulted by my Waiter too because I'm still there without food or any of the other things he told me earlier. And I have already lost four minutes. Too much.

But surprise: my Waiter is not at the station. 'Fuck…'

All our tables are full; he is in the galley, the water jugs missing: I realise that he went to refill them, or more probably someone has stolen them. Also, there is

Angry Waiters   *Federico Fumagalli*

no more bread, I have to take the drinks order (Push for the wine!), one guest needs more butter, the starters here, the main courses there, the Lobsters for the first ones arrived, the salad for the grannies, the soups for the newly married... Shit, shit, I'm in a sea of shit and I haven't started to swim yet.

I think to my own survival skills that work a little bit for everything: though I'm not allowed to, I personally make my own Lobster order on the white docket from the docket pad with the ~~strap-on~~ stripes on it and I come back to Fat Martin, since the other Head Waiters are not in sight. I hope to be luckier this time.

"Hey ya! Look at here, what a nice white docket taken from the docket pad with the stripes on it! Will you sign it?" I say, and I ☺.

Something's wrong again. I can see it. I can see them. I can see the blood veins pumping behind his big ears.

"This is not your Waiter's handwriting! Who did this?! Did you make this?!"

"Yes, I did, because he was in the kitchen..."

"YOU are the one who is supposed to run in and out the kitchen! Not him! He has to stay at the station!"

"I know that, but if you would sign my docket I could carry on with the service, rather than standing here with Passengers on the way to complain, don't you think?" I start to lose my patience.

"Are you telling *me* what to do and how, little boy?!"

"Just sign me the damn paper! Or shall I send you all

Angry Waiters   Federico Fumagalli

the Passengers complaining to you? You are the one in charge, I don't a fuck of them (*or about you*)".

Fat Martin's big ears begin to smoke.

Nobody, never, ever, should talk back to him.

"OK, OK! But now run away, before I give you a warning for your manners!"

'MY manners?' I think.

He signs the docket and I get out of his way. Go back to my station, collect the dirty tray and fly to the kitchen.

That's how long it takes, on average, with the new impeccable rule to improve the service. Really 'complaint-proof'.

I return from the galley with my Lobster, Passengers have something to say about the slow service, to which I reply with an indifferent ☺. My Waiter is furious because we are in such brata that we need a lifeboat, and I slowly start to lose the connections of things to do. I'm really unwilling; there is really no reason to go on like this.

For the following order I have a *bright idea*: I ask my Waiter to make many dockets with 'Lobster' written on it, I look for a Head Waiter with a sense of cooperation who signs all of them, and, time by time, I write the number of Lobsters required.

This is a great idea that allows me to save lot of time, especially because coming soon is the moment of *real* confusion where I have to wash my box and make new mise en place.

Angry Waiters   *Federico Fumagalli*

When I exit the galley to reappear at my station, I find Fat Martin holding my docket pad with the Lobsters already signed by a cooperative Head Waiter.

He looks at me as if it was the last time he sees me alive. He raises the docket:

"Now: what the hell is this?!" he asks me, his face turning dark purple with anger. I look around for my Waiter, who is never in sight when I need him.

"Huuummmm… this looks like the white docket for the Lobster's order…" I murmur, "…with the strap-on it, sorry: with the stripes on it, of course."

"Ya! I can see that! And how come it's already signed?!"

"Because I thought I could save time…"

"You are not paid to think! You have to do what I say, when I say it, as I say it!"

"With all respect, if I do as you say I get in trouble! You are slowing my job. On the other hand, if you let me do as I say…"

No. He doesn't like it.

"Little boy! You better change your behaviour, otherwise it will be a hard time for you! And the signed docket comes with me: who signed it?!"

"A Head Waiter who knows his job!" I reply, and he is about to explode like a supernova, but I'm already light years away from him.

Time goes on, my Waiter gives me pressure, my brain is really switched off for this experience. It's not worth it.

Angry Waiters *Federico Fumagalli*

There are more ~~Fucksters~~ Lobsters to pick up.

And now? Now that I don't have the docket pad?

I guess Fat Martin is going to eat it in the pantry. He's so obese that when he was born, doctors had to perform a caesarean on both of his parents.

Never mind, somehow I manage to steal one docket pad from another station, I write down number '4 Lobsters', I sign it with another pen and a different calligraphy and I jump in the kitchen.

It's done! So easy!

I hand the docket to the Chef.

But he doesn't buy it.

"Who made this?"

"A Head Waiter." I answer seriously.

"This is not his handwriting. Are you sure?"

"There's more than one of them... come on, Chef, please, I'm busy out there!" I beg.

"Be aware I'll check!" he says.

"I don't care! Just move your ass and give me the fucking Lobsters!"

In that moment a Head Waiter comes.

"Hey!" screams the Chef. "Did you sign the docket for the fellow countryman?"

Luckily the three of us are all Italian, and everything *should* be easier.

Should.

I look at the Head Waiter, imploring him with the eyes of the waiter in deep brata. And he answers: "Yes, I signed it. Why? Any problem?"

Angry Waiters   *Federico Fumagalli*

"No, no… because the handwriting is different from usual…"

"Because I signed it in a rush! We don't have time to waste! Give those damn lobsters to Federico!" he shouts, and finally I grab the Lobsters and sauce and with another bounce I'm again at the station. We work directly on the plates making out portions, taking off shells, saucing the pulps and pulping the sauces, when one of the four smart guys asks me: "Excuse me, can I have another one?"

FUUUUCK! I ☺. Another trip in the galley!

Collecting the tray full of dirt and food remains I run to the kitchen, throwing the tray to the Indian dishwashers who in change shout at me different maledictions, then I reappear to the Lobster line to ask "One Lobster alla mano!" which is the rule applied when we need to collect only one plate. I can also jump the queue. Problem is that I realise too late that…

…I don't have the white docket taken from the docket pad with the strap-on it!

"Porca di quella puttana!" I swear (this sounds like *swine that practices sexual services*).

And now? Should I challenge my sad and cynical destiny?

Indeed, the Chef refuses to give me the extra Lobster if I don't hand him the treacherous paper. Signed paper. With-The-Strap-On-It.

At this stage I'm a really angry waiter, and while the queue behind me is waiting and gets longer and I hear complaints about me, I take out from my pocket the light-blue paper that Martin didn't like too much, I turn it back to front and I write down '1 Lobster, You Asshole!', I sign it with my name, I hand it to the Chef, ☺ing, and I grab a Lobster from his hands, a Lobster that he was about to give to somebody else. He begins to scream in South-Englitalian dialect with the laughter of the kilometric queue in the background.

And so on, for the whole night, without dinner because after service there's the Champagne Waterfall.

The following day I will be facing the American Dinner, after which will follow the second of our terrors, the second of our fears, the second of our nightmares:

~~22~~
THE GALLEY ROUND

"Non finisce mai questo giorno del cazzo!" ('There's no end to this cockday!') I repeat loudly in the galley, my legs reaching speeds never seen before.

I'm about to stumble into one of the most absurd and unnerving services of this season, sometimes much more nerve-testing than Lobster Night.

I work together with my Polish Waitress Monika. At first sight she is the ugliest Polish girl of the brigade, but if you look at her a bit more, she's even uglier. Others define her as tough, hard, stressful, unbearable. Others call her Macho Woman. And they kicked me by her side.

Tomorrow we moor at Saint Thomas, a Caribbean island in US territory. Now, each time we dock in US territory, we take the chance to be ambushed by the men of the USPH, who can jump on board at any time to check the hygiene level of every single corner of the ship, and among the brigade terror is unleashed.

I have to arrive on duty even earlier than usual, but now that I know the trick I should bring my hammock and sleep directly at my station.

I arrive and I know that I need to play with more stuff because after dinner there's the Galley Round, where Head Waiters will check that everything (and I really mean *everything*) has been cleaned, hygienised, disinfected, sanitised. Our underwear too.

Angry Waiters   *Federico Fumagalli*

First of all I need to prepare a liquid solution to remove the blackened and oxidised tops of the silver forks: I take my small black box that I usually refill with ice and water and soap, and then I grab a big teapot, holding it firmly with my hands, ready to smash it on the head of whoever tries to steal it. I walk quickly in the galley to prepare this antioxidant acid: I refill the teapot with boiling water and I add a little bit of salt.

Good, here we go. I now need a couple of slices of lemon and some tinfoil.

I walk to the Fruit Station to ask for some lemon slices, but the little bastards don't want to hear anything about lemons for our acid, with the reason that if everybody went to ask them for lemons only to clean their bloody silver forks, they would obviously run out of them within minutes. So, why is it called Fruit Station? Where else can I find lemons? In the Engine Room?

No... Now that I think about it, when I need to serve Iced Teas I can find heaps of fresh lemon wedges at the post of our 'Caffettiere', the man in charge of making hot teas, coffees, cappuccinos... So I carefully walk toward his counter to ask for some... but luckily he is not there, and with the speed of a fox I make four slices disappear.

Two slices are usually more than enough, but my intention is to impress both the Head Waiter and Monika with my super shining forks. Yeah! Let's do this acid properly: let's do it Excellent!

~182~

Angry Waiters   *Federico Fumagalli*

After the lemon theft I need to look for the tinfoil, which I can easily find in the Chef's office. I knock on the door, I cross the forbidden border, I ask if I can *please* take away a *little* piece of tinfoil. After I've made sure that the Chef has forgotten about the day I stole a Lobster from his hands, I wait until he goes back to fill out his paperwork, I grab the roll of tinfoil and very silently I tear away a piece big enough to cover the whole of Mexico, I crumple it into a ball and I push it inside the teapot together with lemon, salt and boiling water. Here you go: the miraculous potion.

Once back at my station I plunge the forks into the teapot, well in contact with the solution, pushing inside the tinfoil ball for a better antioxidation. A few seconds are enough, just the time to make the silver react with salt and tinfoil and make it shining. The job of the lemon is just to remove the smell of the solution on the forks, given that the solution after all stinks really badly. Successively, I rinse the forks in the small black box with water and ice and dry them. If we don't rinse them, the solution can be quite dangerous; it's a poison, so we have to take care. This time I really take this thing seriously, and I rinse and rinse and rinse again, then I go back to the galley to wash the box myself, change water and ice and bring it back.

When I'm done it's time to sort out the salt and pepper containers and the sugar sets. All these I have to refill in the pantry, where sometimes I catch Head Waiters eating a wonderful dinner: they hide plates

Angry Waiters   *Federico Fumagalli*

even behind the coffee machine, behind the bottles of wine, among the bottle spray cleaners. What a big temptation I have of spraying their food with Vetril, Brass polisher, Jiff... but I don't have time. Before going to the pantry I should remember to lock my station, otherwise I better say farewell to all my stuff. I know that on my return something will be missing anyway, in this case my big teapot with the poisonous acid is gone. Vanished. I've been away two minutes, it's my fault: I left it on top of my station.

I lose my temper.

I invoke a divinity that is said to have created the earth and the heavens, begging him to stop copulating with an animal that Muslims can't eat, and start paying attention to me. It doesn't work, so instead I kick down a chair.

I finish the mise en place and sit down for the meeting, without a clue about what kind of chaos tonight will be.

I make good use of the meeting to relax, without even listening to any words, just because they are always the same bullshit: ☺, push for the wine, never say no, be excellent, avoid complaints, run as fast as you can...

I breathe deeply, trying not to be intimidated by the rising pressure among the Crew about the following Galley Round. I know too that it's hard and stressful, but it has to be done *after* work, so why worry too much *before?* I prefer to think about the problem when the time comes, making myself busy only with the

Angry Waiters   *Federico Fumagalli*

coming job. The mistake I make is not to think that there can be other mishaps *during* service too.

First of all I am in one of the two furthest stations from the galley: the reason is that "Fredrico, you are one of the fastest guys I ever seen!"; they noticed that I run very quick – but they didn't get my name right yet – so that I can easily work far away from the kitchen to balance the forces between other stations. What the hell?! Since when does somebody try to work hard and improve himself to reach a target, just to be moved in a more difficult position? Just to make everything harder for him? Only on the Cruise Ship, the *luxury* place for career guys, this can happen. Who am I to discuss it?

Second of all: the new pair of unbreakable shoes bought three weeks ago in Fort Lauderdale are about to break down, and my feet are sore, full of painful blisters which slow my pace. I could compensate the speed by ignoring the pain, but that would mean no ☺, because in order to run with blisters I need to grin my teeth like a hunting dog.

I beg the Goddess of Good Luck to give me a quiet night, but mostly I need the shoes to resist until the end.

End of the meeting, the Headwaiter announces "Sing and Dance!" and we Junior Slaves bounce roaring into the galley for the usual lemon-butter-cheese.

We start again another battling service, but since there are no special events or special menus, lot of people prefer to go up to the Horizon Court. That's

Angry Waiters   *Federico Fumagalli*

good for me, but it doesn't mean anything, indeed after half an hour Monika and I are embraced by Passengers on every table. Our station is full.

The first wave is relatively served in an *excellent* manner, and I start to feel better about the rest of the night. Everything is going all right. Everything's fine. And that should have been the moment to realise that the red alert was ringing in my head, but I didn't. *Everything fine* is a signal of incoming danger.

As soon as the Passengers get up to leave I bring my Big Black Box to be washed, memorising its number: mine is twenty-seven. On each black box (the big one) there is a number that allows us to recognise our own.

After I've done that, comes the time to wash, rinse and sanitise the glasses, obviously in another washing machine. While everything is being cleaned I take advantage of the time to refill my sauce containers, like Horseradish, or the Sour Cream, then the butter with crushed ice, parmesan cheese container; I breathe, I collect my glasses, balance them on a clean tray and go back to the station. People are sitting down like a flow of hungry ants, and since our silverware is counted for twenty people, in my drawers remain the stuff for only two tables. For the other four I need to wait to get my box back. I let Monika know that I'm going to take it and then dry the cutlery in the galley (it's forbidden doing it in the dining room: too noisy).

I walk through the rotating doors and I take a look around: my box is not ready yet. I wait for something

Angry Waiters   *Federico Fumagalli*

to come out from the washing machine, which is rolling continuously, but no box number twenty-seven appears.

I check in the washing machine on the other side of the galley, but there's nothing there too.

"Shit…"

I come back to the left side, asking to my Indian dishwasher friends what happened to my box:

"No box! No box!" they tell me. So where is it? It cannot have disappeared.

Or maybe it can?

I take a worried walk toward Monika, who is ready to strike me with a Macho Woman glance.

"Where is the box!" She says, not as a question, but as a statement. I open my arms gracefully:

"I don't know. It's not in the galley, and I can't find it." I answer with nonchalance.

"What do you mean! Don't tell me you lost it! Did you!" she erupts.

"I don't know! It's not where I've put it! Maybe somebody took it. I don't know!" I say, but she doesn't seem happy with that.

"Go around the dining room and find it!" She commands.

There you go: luxury service my ass, make a career with prof-*ass*-ional people, have a great experience and learn the secrets of a super fine restaurant… The only thing I have learnt until now, besides that 'wedges' is not a brand of apples, and that Always Available is a

~187~

Angry Waiters   *Federico Fumagalli*

dangerous area, is to steal and hide. And not even well enough, since they took my box: the whole box!

Now somebody is enjoying a service with my already deoxidised forks, and my Waitress wants me to search around the whole dining room and check who the guilty bastard is. It's not possible: it was not enough the theft of single items, NO! Now they have to steal the whole box with *all* the items.

I'm not even furious: I just desperately want to give up and leave this place.

Sleeves up to my shoulders, I go.

After the eternity of five minutes I'm back to the dishwashers because maybe, who knows, the box has reappeared from nothingness. But of course not; Monika is super upset with me. My thought is: find a Head Waiter.

Well done, genius! I plead with three Head Waiters, and get the same answer from each one: "It's your business, work it out."

I breathe. I'm really sick of it all and everybody.

I ☺ angrily, the beast counter-attacks. This is war. They want a fight? I will fight.

I come back arrogantly to every single station and, Waiters or no Waiters, I open them and sack whatever I can hold in my hands to be able to prepare the bloody mise en place for my bloody tables on which there are bloody Passengers who demand to have a bloody meal. Monika meanwhile is running back and forth with trays for food, my job.

Angry Waiters *Federico Fumagalli*

I empty my treasure at my station, but it doesn't look like much. No, no: absolutely not, it's not enough. I feel like I want to do another robbing tour passing by the stations that I haven't sacked before. I steal, I take, I rob, I pillage, I ransack everything, whatsoever, from cups to saucers, from cutlery to side plates, breadbaskets, water jugs, a wine opener, a docket pad with stripes on it, a teddy bear, until once more my station takes the shape of a working station, though I still don't have a box.

I'm really angry now; a service cannot carry on this way: but now every Junior Waiter and his dog are gathering around my tables to get back what I've stolen from them. It looks like a riot. They want to steal from me what I've taken from them because they took it from me in first place. It's a never-ending circle. Monika takes place among them to explain the situation, but voices are rising worryingly and a Head Waiter comes to silence everyone.

But by now nobody can stop me, not even with my burning feet, and I fly in the galley once more to the dishwasher – but still, no box – and my obsessed mind takes an evil decision: create chaos among every colleague, friend or not. Or rather: there are no friends in those situations, fuck them all.

I notice around many boxes already washed, none of them carrying the number twenty-seven: I don't give a brata, I take the first one and I refill it taking off items from all the other boxes. Let's see if they learn the

Angry Waiters   *Federico Fumagalli*

lesson.

Each one of my work*mate* protests, but I scream louder and run faster, returning back to my station where Monika watches me holding a treasure that would make a Pharaoh blush.

I camomilize (from Italian slang 'camomillizzare': to make someone calm down, effect of camomile tea) my Waitress who is in crazy brata, but I arrive one second too late: to ruin everything we get a complaint from a bitch of a Passenger with her son of a bitch who writes down on the comment card 'Slow Service'. When the two fuckers leave their table, Monika breaks down in tears. Now: Monika, when she cries, cries full lungs and loud, drawing the attention of a Head Waiter, and while she vents her frustration on me – the evil sent from hell to ruin her life – accusing me because, of course, the cause of all pains is me, I stand in front of her impassive without raising an eyebrow, not taking my eyes off hers. I notify the incoming Head Waiter. Monika gets even more upset because her anger doesn't have the desired effect on me, but I've already lost my patience. All of it. I lose the will to terminate this service, and I'm about to unlace my bow tie, unbutton my vest and walk away leaving her alone in the station, but the Head Waiter convinces me not to do anything stupid. He convinces me not to do anything stupid *but* he *doesn't* help me sort the problem out.

Great!

Angry Waiters   *Federico Fumagalli*

…work with prof-*ass*-ional people…

…learn the secrets of an *excellent* service in the finest dining room of the seven seas...

… ☺ …

OK.

Calm down.

Breathe.

Start everything from the very beginning.

Breathe again, really deep, now everything is going to be OK.

Another deep breath and everything will be all right…

Eh no, Dreamer! Open your eyes!

Here you go: a furious red-haired girl comes with smoking eyes. I think she's Russian. This girl is checking out the box I've stolen in the galley a few minutes earlier. It's *her* box.

Like a duet, she also starts to scream along with Monika, she seems desperate because she came on duty at 16.00 and she had cleaned absolutely every single item of her station for the following Galley Round, and I've scattered them all around my tables, with no mention for the stuff that other Junior Waiters had retaken back on their tables. Maybe the move of this red-haired girl wasn't too smart, because if you wash your silverware *before* duty, *after* duty they won't be so shining and you have to do it again. Maybe her prospect of passing the Galley Round giving the usual happy ending to the checking Head Waiter would

Angry Waiters Federico Fumagalli

have worked, but for tonight I have ruined her mood.

Since the box was stolen from me, I did the same. I grab the Russian and bring her in the galley to check once more: I'm sorry, dear friend, No Box! She goes mad, yelling at me; I go nuts too, and get enraged with her.

Her mistake is to try to put her hands on me. I block her. This time I scream to her, and in my life this is the first and only time I've ever raised my voice and behaved angrily to a lady.

"Woman or not", I shout at her, "I don't give a shit about you! I kick your ass and bring you back to your country – whatever it is – to work on the street! Join your mum!"

"You fucking Italian! You and your Mafia always fooling around and fucking and stealing! You come here and think you are the best! You are the best of shit! One contract, promotion! Another contract, another promotion! Go back in your mother's pussy and…"

Only the rushing appearance of the Head Waiter saves her from a heavy headbutt on her nose.

He shuts her up and shouts at me to return to my station. He shouts at me to return to the station but he doesn't help me to sort this out.

It seems to me that the latest fashion on board is shouting at me and letting me drown in my own brata; it'must be written on every adult XXX magazine, since every wanker is doing it.

~192~

Angry Waiters   *Federico Fumagalli*

As I set foot in my station, the shit is submerging us: even a cargo with toilet paper rolls wouldn't save us. But surprise of all surprises… My box number twenty-seven is standing on top of the working table. Reappeared!

Empty, but reappeared. Who brought it back, I will never know. I take the chance to give back the box to the red-haired girl, not before taking off it some other little gift, and then I carry on with my job trying in vain to regain the time lost.

At 22.00 doors close down.

It's finished. It's the end. I can relax.

Relax…?

Finished…?

I can almost hear it…

Yes, my ears are hearing it…

"The guy from Cremella takes this Caramella!" Someone says.

My blood red eyes jump off my face to take a closer look at the Head Waiter who has sat the last couple on my tables. It's really true: there is no end to this cockday.

The last table of the night… to me. I raise my eyes to the ceiling and I clench my fists. Monika gets upset with the Head Waiter, who in turn replies: "Today you, tomorrow somebody else!"

"Yeah… depends if *you* survive until tomorrow." I whisper.

If it weren't for all those CCTV cameras I would

Angry Waiters   *Federico Fumagalli*

crash and burn the whole dining room and everyone in it.

While everyone else is clearing away their stations for the main disinfection, I have to bear the last loving couple.

We should wait until every single Passenger at our station has left before we can carry on with our sanitisation, and we are the only ones who still can't move a finger. But at this stage Monika and I realise that if we follow this strict rule we won't get to sleep before 01.00, so we declare a temporary *truce* and I suggest an idea. She agrees with that and she ☺s. I have never seen her smiling, although it doesn't make her look any better.

Tension lowers a bit, and after ten seconds of *total* break I return under the effort of my usual striking pace. My feet hurt.

I put in action my own method of following the rules, sanitising tables even with the loving couple still sitting and eating, so that they quickly understand that they are not so well accepted.

I throw everything I have in my black box making the most of noise: plates, cups, chinaware, cutlery, coffee pots, teddy bears… and I bring it to the dishwashers. I show them my eyes and my fingers pointing to them, meaning that I'm watching and stalking every single move of the box *and* themselves. If the box vanishes, so will they. Then I wash the glasses and I bring them back to the station holding them with my fingers

Angry Waiters   *Federico Fumagalli*

because at the moment there are no clean trays available; this is punishable with a hundred lashes.

I bounce back in the galley to keep an angry eye on my box number twenty-seven, nobody is going to fuck with me from now on. As it comes out of the rolling washing machine I jump on it and set-up a guard. I move it onto the big long table (which is not large enough to contain the whole box: the edge underneath crosses the border of the table, so people running may stumble on them, throwing everything on the floor) and I dry and divide the cutlery. I put the clean tray with the cutlery balanced on the box and I bring it to my station. The loving couple is still sitting there, talking and caressing hands and calling each other with stupid loving nicknames and making all those annoying things that couples do on a dining table except for getting off on it, so for inducing them to move their ass out of there I keep waving and shaking all my tablecloths like a chequered flag at a Grand Prix. My effort is really worth it. They get the message that I don't care that much of their presence, and they finally go to play nurse and patient in their room.

From now on Monika and I have to carry on with our sanitisation task: we have to dismantle the cutlery containers from their respective drawers and wash them; pass the blue towel wet with chlorine even inside the corners of the armchairs to eliminate any possible breadcrumbs, then passing the same towel on any possible and imaginable surface visible by human eye

Angry Waiters   *Federico Fumagalli*

and touchable by *in*human hands, outside and inside the station's working table, every movable part, every standing surface, in and out, over and under, left and right. She takes care of the station, I take care of the silverware.

For this task I have to set foot in the galley with whatever is made of silver: breadbaskets, sugar sets, teapots and coffee pots, creamer, ice buckets, stands for ice buckets, cheese containers, salt and pepper corks, and god knows what.

Every single piece has to be rubbed thoroughly with a special 'silver paste' and a sponge, and then have to be rinsed. After that it will be given to the dishwashers who then sterilise it in the washing machine at a temperature of seven thousand degrees Celsius, Fahrenheit and Richter.

Once everything is excellently clean – around half an hour or more – I bring everything back to the station and I vigilantly dry all the dangerous drops of water, because if a Head Waiter checks and finds a single drop of vapour on the glass lid of the cheese container, it's not enough that I dry it up: no, I have to wash it again. If a Head Waiter checks and finds a breadcrumb on the chair, it's not enough that I push it away: no, I have to wrap a knife with a blue towel and go deep down inside the back and the seat of it. And of course, he is not waiting for me: when I'm done I need to go around and call him again for a second check.

When, and if we are given the OK, Monika sets

~196~

Angry Waiters *Federico Fumagalli*

everything back at the station, and I come back to the galley because something is wrong: my teapots and coffee pots, this time. Coffee pots and teapots have to be washed with chlorine on the inside. With the silver paste outside, with the chlorine inside: what the hell...

When it's all finally fine – though I think nothing is ever fine enough for them... but of course, stupid me: it has to be Excellent! – and the Headwaiter has checked everything once more, we set all our super shining stuff in our super shining station and we close it with a super shining lock. I keep the key, because the day later I come on duty again before my Waitress. This big time-wasting job has to be done three nights a week, each time we are about to approach any of the US docks. And three times a week I have to fight with my work*mates* to get a blue towel, for a spoonful of silver paste, for a little space on a working table for rubbing and cleansing.

None of the above is usually enough for everybody, and I rarely can get the three of them all together. Sometimes I manage to get the blue towel and silver paste, but no space at all on the table, so I have to wait until someone has disappeared. Or if I have space on the table and have the blue towel, I may not have got hold of silver paste, and occupying space on the table just makes other people angry because I'm therefore wasting their time. Not that I care anyway.

Also, I need to hope that nobody mistakes my already deoxidized forks with their own blackened ones,

Angry Waiters   *Federico Fumagalli*

otherwise there is a new magical potion to prepare, and the chef's office at this time is closed and I can't get the tinfoil.

But I have a solution for everything: in the following days, cooperating with my room-mate Robert M, I will be able to attempt the Tinfoil Theft directly in the chef's office. What we need would be: alertness, eyes open, ears open, and my magic wine opener to unlock the door. There you go. The whole tinfoil roll is in our hands and in our cabin. Always Available!

From that day and afterwards, each time we come on duty, we just need to open our drawer in our cabin, crumple a little piece of magic shining paper, and go to steal the first big teapot we can get hold of. Simple, isn't it?

Finally the duty for this Galley Round ends. I'm drained, my feet burning, my blisters on the way to explosion, I'm unmotivated, I'm terribly hungry, nervous, and I really need to sleep.

But I can't: tonight again it's Champagne Waterfall night!

I check in the noticeboard what could be my task, but I can't find my name on there.

Because…

…Yeah! I'm on the Dining Room shift! Champagne Waterfall is done by Lido Lunch people! Ah, such luck!

But even so, there's something I have to do but seems like I forgot about it. What the hell was that? I hope it

Angry Waiters   *Federico Fumagalli*

was nothing important; with all the chaos I have been through, my brain deleted it.

I march through the galley holding the dishes of my stolen dinner, cold, and the ice cream, melted, and I meet Aneta who in turn gives me the thumbs up: 'Are you coming up to the Crew Bar later on?' and at that moment I realise what I have forgotten: I was supposed to meet with Agata, a wonderful blonde Polish girl who works at Crew Bar for a walk on the ~~dick~~ deck, under the stars. She is one of the newly embarked, a new work bee, and sometimes when we are not so shattered after work we take a drink. She is Assistant Bar Girl, one or two levels under the Junior Slave.

She recently earned the position of *hornithologist,* therefore I'm doing my best to introduce her a new species of bird.

On my ugly face appears a big ☺, thinking to the happy ending of this night, and I walk down the stairs to reach the Crew Mess, but suddenly the sole of my right shoe comes off at the second step leaving the naked wood to get grip on the next step. The thing is… the wood doesn't get any grip at all on a wet step…

As I touch the third step, I slip and my leg turns upwards, while my body falls downwards through the staircase, rolling down with my dinner plates which surprisingly go to hell. Forever.

Everything crashes and bangs around me. When I reach the bottom I call for a Goddess who usually mates with grunting mythological creatures that after

Angry Waiters   *Federico Fumagalli*

death become sausages.

Two chefs come to see what happened, while I'm counting all the saints of heaven. As if it wasn't funny enough, the Indian dishwashers get mad at me because now they have to wash the staircase again. They also make me feel guilty of having rolled down. The chefs disappear as soon as I get on my feet. Nobody has the friendly idea of asking me if I'm OK, or hurt, or whatever. The Indian dishwashers stand there waiting for me to go away as quick as possible, but no one thinks about helping me. I pick up my shoe sole; I *apologise* for having fell, and walk away, furious. Amok. Blindly irate. One of them also has the politeness of asking me: "Hey boy: you forgot something, don't you?"

I turn my head, just to see him pointing at the broken plates and the food littering the floor. "Who is gonna clean this mess?" the Indian dishwasher asks me, with a tone that I don't really like.

I carry on toward the Crew Mess, waving my hand and raising him a very big middle finger.

In the Crew Mess my other Italian work*mates* have already finished their stolen meals, and in the Crew's buffet there is absolutely nothing left. Not even a bread roll. I drink a Fanta and I walk to my grave to take a shower, still holding my broken sole in my hands. I'm so hungry I wish I could eat it.

What a fuck-up of a day! But there's still Agata ☺…

I take the lift up to the Crew Bar, Deck 8, looking for

her. At the beginning I can't find her – I'm a little bit late – but then I meet Aneta who tells me that she saw Agata on the other side of the lounge, sitting on the comfortable armchairs together with her girlfriends. I walk toward them, trying to find a reason for my lateness, but she is not even among them. They tell me she is already gone to bed.

What I don't like is *with whom* they tell me she is gone to bed...

I hate him and he hates me.

He's a F&B.

He is tall and bald.

And he is Austrian.

Agata took the wrong bird, though I'm sure it ended up in the proper nest.

With winds of war in my heart I have nothing else left but to go back to my cabin, thinking about what sort of revenge, harsh or bitter, I might take on him.

He will pay for this.

With interest.

Angry Waiters   *Federico Fumagalli*

~~23~~
WINE TASTING AND TIME WASTING

For the ones on the two weeks Dining Room shift, they sometimes happen to get the honour of being on duty some more and have something else to do.

How is it possible to have time to exploit extra work, when normally time is missing? On board time is compressed as if it was an MP3 file, to make sure that in twenty-four hours we work forty-eight.

Wine Tasting is done by Waiters. So lucky I am! I am Junior Slave! I *don't* have to be on duty after Lunch from 15.00 to 16.30! I *don't* have to remain in the dining room on a continuous circle listening to rivers of blurring words dictated by Head Waiters and Passengers, made half-drunk by the dozen glasses of wine that they taste. Multicolour glasses everywhere, just to induce the Passenger into temptation of buying a bottle for the night and increase the revenue.

I *don't* have to note on a white paper taken from the docket pad with the strap-on it, the cabin number and the wine's bottle number, chosen by the Passenger, and the day before I *don't* have to walk around the ship trying to sell tickets for this great opportunity that is the Wine Tasting – because if you think it's given for free, you're wrong.

But when I come on duty at 16.30, as usual, I find total chaos: heaps of glasses still to be rewashed – if I'm lucky – heaps of glasses missing or shattered on

Angry Waiters   *Federico Fumagalli*

the floor – if I'm unlucky – drawers and little doors of the station wide open with high chance of getting multi-theft at my own cost... and I have to change all tablecloths, clean the chairs, *find* the chairs scattered around the dining room with the same pattern on each table... get back what I don't have any more by checking in other stations.

But if I'm Junior Waiter and I don't have to do the Wine Tasting, what is it that I have to do?

~~24~~
TEATIME

Everybody on board knows that among the ones who hate the Teatime, I am the one who hates it most.

Really: I hate it with all my heart. I would gladly perform an extra Galley Round rather than being present with Teatime duty from 15.00 to 16.30, especially because I finish Lunch shift just a few minutes before Teatime, after that I put in action the rockets on my feet – with the new pair of unbreakable shoes I bought – to rush in my cabin, change uniform and wear the horrible white gloves. At 16.29 I must re-fly in my cabin and re-change uniform, sometimes I do not even have time to shower, I re-put gel on my hair and I re-jump to dining room at 16.31 – impossible for many, but not for all – risking that in two minutes every item would be wiped away. And in the meanwhile I haven't got any food down my stomach.

I start dinner with the increasing impression that soon I will become cannibal and I will feed on work*mates*, or I will become vegetarian and I will munch apple wedges.

Teatime – here is the almost good news – is one of those little tasks that I can choose not to perform: I just need to pay somebody else to do it for me, but it's not as cheap as the Napkin Folding: Napkin Folding is fifteen dollars; Teatime costs twenty-five dollars, and it has to be done twice a week, for two weeks. This

Angry Waiters Federico Fumagalli

makes a bunch of one hundred lost bucks if I want to recover a few hours of sleep, which are, in two weeks, less than four. Sleep is more valuable than gold.

The performance of today's Teatime, by my side, is not a superb one.

So: I finish Lunch at 14.56 because I obviously take Caramellas a go-go, and I skip my lunch. I start-up the shoe's turbojet, I arrive in my cabin, I throw my uniform on the bed, I change uniform, I flow out the door like a thundering river, I leap to the top of the staircase's thirteen steps with one only jump, I turn the corner and I crash against the sternum of a F&B Manager: guess which one?

Yes: the Austrian.

The tall and bald one.

The one that slept with Agata…

He goes furious.

I leave him there with all his fury while he's shouting something at me in Austrian, and beating the speed record 'Bow to Stern' I manage to arrive in the dining room in time to realise that the Teatime has already begun.

The Head Waiter strikes me with a glance, I feel almost guilty; looking around among the colleagues I am the only Italian.

So, while I'm recovering my breath, and my tongue is quadruple its size, I try to find an excuse for my lateness, which I can't find.

The Head Waiter grabs my arm and explains to me

Angry Waiters   *Federico Fumagalli*

what my task consists of. For me it's all the same, whatever it is I feel bad. I feel shame. That kind of service is not for me. I can't make myself like it.

Could I be the one who serves hot water for tea and coffee? No.

Could I be the one who serves pastries? No.

Could I be the one who serves scones? No.

Could I be the one who... No.

Could I be the... No.

Could I... No.

Cou... No.

No, No, and NO! – Why NOT?

I am the one who passes around with a tray, on top of which there is Jam and Sweet Cream, waiting for the others to serve their pastries and scones. When they are done, it's my turn to ask: "Would you like Jam or Sweet Cream? On top or on the side (of the scones)?" and so on, with a fake ☺ on my lips and true curses in my head, wishing not to invert the two things.

My discomfort increases when it comes to repeat the tour around the tables, when I have to ask again to everybody, each one of them, one by one, if they want to get fatter and fatter with some "Jam or Sweet Cream? On top or on the side?" and nobody wants any more of the above.

Then the Head Waiter asks me to go around again, for the third time, terrified that a Passenger might place a complaint to him because he/she didn't have enough Jam or Sweet Cream on top or on the side.

Angry Waiters   *Federico Fumagalli*

After I've asked the same thing three times, and each time each Passenger refused my 'Jam or Sweet Cream! Come on!' I start to feel a complete idiot. But the Head Waiter insists. What? Once more?!

I'd love so much to hammer the Head Waiter's testicles with the power of my angry fist, and shout him that 'Nobody wants any more of your stupid Sweet Cream!!!!'

During one of those Teatimes I apprehend that Passengers are insuperable cretins: I'm referring now to their idea of Sexual Harassment. For being Italian, I have to be very careful. They complain for things that for us are absolutely normal. How would I know if I hadn't experienced it myself?

I can't give to an American woman an obvious lascivious look: she could easily report me to the police just because she doesn't like the way I look at her, especially if she's wearing something sexy, or simply attractive. Why don't you stay in your cabin, then?

I'm following the guy with the scones, still holding my tray with Jam and Cream and without noticing it – OK, I admit: I am deliberately doing it – I find myself looking through the neckline of the breast of a quite attractive woman in her thirties. Her two tits inside a black transparent dress make their good figure: they are bright and round with two nipples waiting just to be hailed.

I am already imagining myself spreading the left one

Angry Waiters   *Federico Fumagalli*

with Jam and the right one with Cream, when she shouts: "Hey! *Where* are you looking at?!"

I freeze like a fool, incapable to decide whether or not to find an answer or pretend nothing happened.

Unfortunately my face blushes so much it turns red like her nipples; she has caught me straight and guilty.

This happened once, years ago, when I was studying in a Professional Hospitality School in Italy when, during a school meeting, I got caught by my English teacher staring at the legs of another sexy teacher who was wearing a very short skirt, waiting for her to criss-cross her legs.

"Fumagalli?! You are not paying much attention, are you?"

"I was, until now..."

On board, same situation.

But, I mean, you poor woman that comes to the Teatime: you arrive with a neckline that seems a tit's showcase, your boobs up in the air free and happy like a butterfly, and then you don't want that we entomologists stand there evaluating the species?

Nevermind. This will be one of my last Tea Times; from now on I'll pay twenty-five dollars to someone and to hell with everybody. I can't even hear any more this annoying small orchestra's music! No more!

I'm leaving the room, I escape because I still have to take a shower and change my uniform once more, and while I walk out I meet a couple that I happily served the night before: they gladly greet me hoping to be paid back with a best friend's ☺, but I can't give them this satisfaction because just in that moment I'm trying to swallow a big block of snot that is obstructing my throat. They stand there, waiting for me to wave my hand.

But it's not going to happen.

~~25~~

IN PORT MANNING AND SEXUAL EMBARRASSMENT

I'm having an erotic dream where all the ladies are covered with Nutella and I'm the only slices of bread in the room, when suddenly...

TRRRR... TRRRR... TRRRRRRRRRR...

WHAT!

THE!

HELL!

MHHH! My vibrator (I still mean the vibrations from my mobile phone)! Where did I put it this time?! Hell... The light! Where's the light?! Where's the phone?! Where am I?!! Where are the girls?! Why am I still alive?!?

OK, quick wake up and brain into gear: today is Saturday, Turnaround day: I start working earlier even than Breakfast shift because today there is Passenger disembarkation and re-embarkation.

Let's get rid of all the old ones, and let the new two thousand eight hundred come on in.

More ferocious and hungrier than the previous wave.

Today I *could* be *off*, which means I *could* be free from 10.00 to 16.00.

I could go to sleep.

I could go to Fort Lauderdale.

I could go to the beach.

Angry Waiters *Federico Fumagalli*

I could go to Miami.

But I can't even go screw myself because I'm once more on that duty called 'In Port Manning' and I am in the Embarkation Team. The one with the white gloves.

First of all I'd like to explain what the In Port Manning is: it's something that *nobody* loves to do, but it has its utility.

When I am doing In Port Manning my Laminex is withdrawn and I *cannot* go out any more. Without this card I am condemned to remain on board. Why is that?

Because if there was an emergency on board and everybody was off duty and inland, who would face the danger? Who would take care of our lovely Passengers?

To ensure their safety and well-being, the company needs to keep somebody on board who could possibly save their life; somebody *brave* and *fearless*; somebody who is *not* scared of lifting heavy weights; somebody *reliable;* somebody who *cares* of them.

Somebody like *me*.

☺?!?

This week I am *The Chosen One*. Not alone, of course, but I feel the responsibility of two thousand eight hundred lives depending on me, and that puts a grin on my face. A grin of vengeance of course!

My role is APP (Assistant Passenger Party), and in case of a real emergency I should transport injured or disabled Passengers by using wheelchairs or stretchers. Those stretchers are built to last, but most importantly

Angry Waiters   *Federico Fumagalli*

have been designed to give the chance for us to bring Passengers up and down the stairs thanks to special wheels attached on their lower part. They have been thinking big time about wheels: seeing how much these people weigh, who would lift them?

The problem indeed is not the transportation, but the effort of setting them on the stretchers, or on the wheelchairs which are kept on the stern of the ship.

But now I don't care: I'm in In Port Manning, I can't get out, and I have to start my Embarkation Team's duty.

One more time, I am the one who indicates the way to the new intruders that don't know where to go. Without me, they are totally lost (but also *with* me, if I think back to the last time I did it, when I blocked the flow of people at the Art Gallery: it's not my fault. I speak their language, maybe not at the highest level, but they understand what they want to understand, and they act consequently).

Last time I was super late, so this time I want to impress every Supervisor arriving to the 11.30 duty ten minutes earlier.

I get there at 11.20 and I realise that I'm twenty minutes *late*. The shift begun at 11.00; it seems that this thing never reaches the links of my brain.

As the Supervisor finishes with the huge *ronzata*, as a punishment he puts me in the worst position, even worse than doggy style with me in the front: the position is the initial one, right next to him so he can

Angry Waiters   *Federico Fumagalli*

put his eyes on me. I know he would be glad to put something else in me, because he is gay. He has already tried once, but failed.

It's the worst position if you think that Passengers, as they cross the line and they put one foot on board, *want* a fresh and pure ☺; *pretend* imperial and joyful welcoming; *demand* answers to questions they haven't asked yet.

How is all this possible? This is the secret of the Super Waiter.

But talking about serious things, me – being a hunter male – I am only interested at looking at all the pretty girls coming along with their new two thousand eight hundred friends: I ☺ to them, they ☹ back to me; I greet them, they greet me back; I welcome them, they tell me to piss off.

I scrupulously watch: breast when they enter; face and eyes when they get closer; thighs when they walk past me; miniskirt and ass when they start running far away from me, toward the Art Gallery.

When they approach in a group, my sight becomes sharper; my look becomes malicious; my cheeks give my stupidity away; the girl's pace gets quicker.

They come and go, come and go, and my imagination flies… until the Landing Tower of the Erotic Dreams announces: 'Sexual Harassment! Sexual Harassment!' and the prison appears with the sign 'Next →'

If imagination doesn't fly, it can easily navigate on the waves, until an ugly guy surrounded by his belly

~213~

Angry Waiters   *Federico Fumagalli*

asks me where he can find the buffet. I'd like to say: *'You've entered the ship fifteen metres ago, and you are already hungry?!'* but I can't, of course I can't, so I carry on repeating: 'On this way!' and I send him towards the lifts.

Every time a nice girl walks in front of me, I have this strong temptation of moving one hand on my crotch and shouting "On *this* way!" with the other hand, but I'm already in a dangerous position.

Here we can be disembarked straight away.

There's no way to survive if you get caught after having had sex (or even worse: *while* having sex) with a Passenger in one of their cabins: first there is a big Warning (though here there's a warning for everything, even when things go well, because they should go Excellent!); then there is a trial to which the Captain will surely take part; at the end, disembarkation takes place. Thrown at sea for sharks' breakfast.

If the woman is Bastard, and this happens often, she can charge you for any of the following: malicious look from your side (Sexual Harassment); a word way too much over the edge (Sexual Harassment); an eye blinking too much (Sexual Harassment); a letter too written (Sexual Harassment, black on white).

On the other side, if the woman is a Super Bastard, then we are in trouble. The Super Bastard woman gets on board just and only to fuck with whoever still manages to get it hard, especially among waiters and

~214~

Angry Waiters Federico Fumagalli

barmen, which I consider the horniest human species on the globe.

This woman doesn't need to receive proposals: she chooses. She is the hunter.

Usually she can count on her attractiveness, allowing herself to fool around half naked for two purposes:

1– To generate envy among wives of Passengers

2– To create attention among Crew Members.

That said, she usually doesn't get herself in trouble with Passengers or boyfriends; she prefers to get in trouble somebody else: the Crew. Thanks to her body appearance she can act however she likes, ninety-nine per cent sure that no one would dare to say 'NO!' (Never say NO! is our brand standard) to her advances. She knows that to the Crew is forbidden to have sex with Passengers, and that's why she acts carelessly: it's the feeling of prohibition that excites her.

Once she has chosen her pray, she acts.

Once the pray falls for her grace, end of career.

She gathers her man into her sexual trap and then (this has really happened, and I couldn't believe myself when I heard about it), after she had shaken him for the whole night, she walks down to reception and she *places a complaint* because *he* hasn't been satisfying enough. Not only *has he made* a very embarrassing impression with her: he made it with all his colleagues too. Word spreads out as quickly as the high tide, and he had risked to be disembarked. Also, at the reception desk there are the Officials too, and the other girls will

~215~

never look at him any more.

Sexual Harassment for ladies, Sexual *Embarrassment* for gentlemen: that's the sad truth.

~~26~~
TIPS

On board we survive thanks to the TIPS. We don't have salary, and if there is one, it is absolutely derisory: mine is *thirty dollars* per month. One dollar per day. Better say that our salary is made of tips.

Once, a long time ago, Passengers used to give envelopes with tips to servers, to share between Head Waiters, Sommeliers, Waiters, and Junior Waiters. The higher the position, the higher the tips.

To the present day remains unchanged the story of the position, but tips are now *automatic*. The Passenger, at the end of the cruise, will see his Cruise Card's Credit being devolved in charity to the staff.

This way, there shouldn't be any danger that Passengers run away without leaving something for us. Unfortunately, that's not *so* true: the Passenger still has the option to cancel our tips in case he hasn't been fully satisfied of our efforts to make him happy. If the tip gets cancelled in our department, we get filled up with the same stories of *'Sometimes you said NO! You didn't push for the wine! You didn't smile enough! You didn't run as quickly as you could have!'* and so on; useless to say that it doesn't have any effect on us. For us, the real guilty entity for the cancellation of our tips is the *Passenger's brain*.

A Passenger is entitled to cancel our tips for any reason, even the most stupid one.

Angry Waiters   *Federico Fumagalli*

It happens to me to see tips cancelled for unbelievably little details, and sometimes I get bad comments on the Comment Cards located on each table. But I don't care too much (*we* don't care too much) because we know which level of IQ our Passengers are. Moreover, I do my best every time, so if sometimes I make mistakes, who cares: it happens to everyone.

If it's really my fault, head down. If I made everything possible, the complaint can easily go to hell.

Let alone the complaint of the woman and her son who gave me a complaint for 'Slow Service' when my box was stolen, usually tips are cancelled for a problem called 'Stingy Passenger'.

A good example is this lady with black crow's hair, aquiline nose, goose bumps, and web-footed fingers: I sit her at the table, I pull the chair back, I push it forward, I open the menu for her, I serve water from the water jug, and then I ask her about the drinks. Well, she asks me annoyingly for which reason I didn't open the napkin in a triangle shape on her lap as all the other waiters have done before: maybe I thought she doesn't deserve an *excellent* service?

~~Of course she doesn't~~ Of course she does!

OK, I confess, I'm guilty: I didn't open the napkin. But that's only because I am in total brata in the middle of my duty, and I am trying to make everybody happy and I'm pushing and running and ☺ing. I simply forget

Angry Waiters   *Federico Fumagalli*

that one little detail. I apologise and rush to pick up her napkin, but on the comment card she writes 'Low' in the Service, writing down my name 'Frederico', which I suggest her to review because it's wrong, indeed it is 'Federico' (I spell it out for her), but then she looks at me as if I thought she weren't able to read my name badge.

Sorry again: I keep forgetting that my name on the badge is still wrong: so I actually tell her that she is not able to read, when indeed she is reading my wrong name properly.

Another couple, instead, I welcome in an exemplar manner: I make triangles and origami of napkins and everything else, but then, still struggling to fight the Battle for the Tips at my station field, I have to concentrate on the other tables too.

A couple of minutes later the man stands up pointing his finger to me. I raise my hands thinking he wants to shoot a complaint, and I think right because he asks me: "Do we have to wait some more before you serve us water?!", so I answer: "I'm really sorry (yeah…yeah…)! I'll serve you *immediately!*".

I wait until he is seated, I turn, look at my water jugs, and my lungs stop breathing: all of them are empty. Fuck! I fly to refill them in the galley, but on my return I find my Waiter dealing with them, their voices quite loud. Ten seconds later, they stand up from their chairs and walk out. Another complaint on the comment card, and just for a drop of water! I can't believe how

Angry Waiters   *Federico Fumagalli*

mentally retarded some people can be!

Then obviously my Waiter has this idea of shouting at me angrily because I didn't serve water *immediately*, and I explain that among the thousands things I had to do, I was able to do only nine hundred and ninety-nine, and I'm still there with the three water jugs in my hands. (By the way: where was *he*?)

He repeats that I *must not* answer back to him and that I have to be faster and bla, bla, bla, and while the river of words is flowing out his mouth, I have the unbearable will of accidentally dropping my iced water on him.

Who cares? Him, as a Waiter, can't scream and make bad impressions among the tables, while me, Junior Slave, has nothing to lose, especially after having announced that I will voluntarily disembark within the next few months.

Another lost tip comes from a couple that I can't easily recognise as a 'couple', meaning man and woman. I take them in my hands, I welcome them to my table, I sing the National Anthem, I throw rose petals at their feet, I say "Good evening, Madame" to the lady, and then "Good evening, Sir" to the other person.

Big mistake.

My tired eyes hadn't notice something…

Suddenly, the one I called 'Sir' threatens me with a furious look: "How dare you call me *Sir*?! I'm a *Lady*!"

Angry Waiters   *Federico Fumagalli*

Lady? I'm sorry for her, but… with such short hair, small moustache, no breasts at all, jeans and slippers, a principle of beard on her cheeks… I can hardly recognise her as a woman.

I try to apologize: "Oh, I'm sorry, Sir…"

"Again! I told you I'm a Lady! Lady! Understand?"

"Yes, yes, yes, Sir.. Sorry… Madame!"

"AAAAAHHHH!"

She yells too much, and I suddenly feel everyone's eyes stuck on me.

Another complaint to add to my sad collection, department 'Lack of Respect', and of course the tip is deducted from the already unhappy quote.

Other times it seems like things could get better and we take *extra* tips that don't make any difference for us. Unless, of course, only if we can get them back from the Head Waiter.

If Passengers are happy about service and they ask to come back tomorrow to be served by the same Waiter and Junior Slave, it's a good sign. But considering the elements, it's easy to fall in the trap. Usually, we underpaid *'dish-bringers',* get screwed in two basic ways: A and B.

Number A: Passengers come to us *every* night except for Friday, which is the last day of the cruise and they know is the 'tipping day'. This way we work our ass hard and at the end we don't see a dollar.

Number B: Passengers come *every* day of the week, even on Friday which is the last day and it's called

American Night in their honour, and they know it is the day when they must open their dear wallets. End of the dinner, happy and ☺ing, they stand up and shake our hands, a pat on the shoulder, occasional picture and lot of well-wishing for our career. This way we work even harder, and at the end of the fairy tale we don't see a dollar.

We look at them, still ☺ing big time because they have been fooling us the whole week, and then we carry on with our duty, full of apprehension.

But still… this is not enough. To my Waiter and me happens the case of 'Artistic but Useless Tips'.

I still remember them, each one of them, one uglier than the other.

Old, fat, and (more dangerous) single. Wrinkles try to escape off their face, but they are kept on the skin by an inch of make-up and glue.

Those eight old maids are engulfing themselves with food. I can hear their jaws crunching and munching a mixture of prawn and onion soup and lobster and whatsoever, even egg shells. They are the kind of women that once conquered a coffee table they'll never leave it for the rest of the day. They would nail their fat buttocks to it, and that's it. End of the story. They are the classic Teatime lovers. Nothing to say about that; better them than me.

This little bunch of bad-luck-bringer ladies gather in social levels just and only to talk silly behind the back of We Men, perpetrators of god knows what kind of

Angry Waiters Federico Fumagalli

sentimental denigration at their cost. They complain and denigrate us without mercy, no respect whatsoever. I suppose they don't want to declare their lesbian status, and I genuinely fear them. Them, and their straps-on.

My Waiter and I, an Italian one this time (Monika refused to keep working with me, and she begged the Head Waiters to get rid of my corpse – she even offered her sexual availability spontaneously, but they all refused), have our station half taken up by them: they asked for a table of twelve people, but only eight appeared. Better off like that. Those harlots are always ready to make fun of us as soon as we turn our backs, but they don't know that we do the same to them. They all dress in a disgusting way, with clothes Nostradamus didn't even consider in his predictions.

I turn to the fattest and ugliest, ☺ing of course, and I say to my Waiter: "Don't you think that the one sitting on the top table, with the long bushy hat, looks like Otelma the Wizard?"

My Waiter bursts out in laughter.

(Otelma in Italy is a famous wizard who always tries to do magic under his Divine Intervention, his Occult Sense and his loyal trust in Paranormal Superpowers. All his efforts, anyway, are always vain; he really can't perform anything, but he looks really serious in his little shows. Although he tries to convince people that he can speak with the Dead, his Superpowers have never shown up on television; electric circuits are to be

Angry Waiters   Federico Fumagalli

blamed, because they create interference with his hypnotic mind, and can be dangerous for *his* health. Well, from how he dresses up – long large gowns, long, large bushy stupid hats, colourful but mystic long sleeves – he has a lot of similarities with an incapable clown. And the lady I'm talking about really looks like him, especially for her make-up and size).

This lady wants to know why we are laughing, but her facial expression is horrifying to me, and to avoid laughing at her face – the way you would do when you see a monkey who can't peel a banana – I run in the galley with their order.

A very difficult order: one of them is vegetarian but can eat *salmon*; one is vegan but can still perform *oral*; one is diabetic but can drink *Sprite*; one wants a steak *rare, but make sure is well cooked inside;* one is constipated but allergic to *prunes;* one wants spaghetti bolognese but without *minced meat;* one wants Iced Tea but she wants it *hot;* one wants a consommé, but just *one slice*.

The Chef refuses even to insult me after I hand him the order.

"Why not a *Dick's Soup* for everyone?" he shouts at me.

At the end of the week those ladies hand us an envelope with a few dollars inside. I must say that regardless of their habit and appearance, they have received from us a service that went beyond excellence; crossed the borders of perfection and

Angry Waiters   *Federico Fumagalli*

expectation; exceeded the horizons of unbelievableness. We had them have a bit of fun by mixing Italian and English, teaching them some useful phrases, and giving them little tips and advice on how to recognise and hook up with romantic Italian men, but if they have a crumb of brain hopefully they'll never use any of our teachings.

Attached to the envelope there is a little *poem* about the two of us (poem whose words I'm glad I forgot). They are very disappointed about leaving, while I can't contain my happiness.

After they are gone, we check inside of the envelope, that usually should be handed to the Head Waiter which will give it us back on Sunday, if its contents hasn't been used to fill some hole here and there of the cancelled tips (and, surprise, surprise: it happens every week).

But this envelope has something special; I'd say something magic and mystic.

We prefer not to give it to anyone. Better not to tell anyone what's inside, we have a reputation to keep.

There are six dollars inside (to share between two), but it's not the quantity…

It's the *way* they put them inside…

We feel shame to hand it to the Head Waiter, so my Waiter suggests me to keep it deep down in my pocket and keep my mouth very shut.

"Burn it!" Is his comment.

After the dinner, that today I managed to steal in

Angry Waiters   *Federico Fumagalli*

exaggerated proportion and I'm happy like a kid on Easter Day holding a giant chocolate egg, I hide in my little cabin and check the work of those old maids: the six dollars are useless because they are *folded* and *sewn* together as an origami, forming the shape of a *working shirt*!

Where's the number of the Mental Hospital?!

But what can I say… What can I do!

I just hope the next Passengers won't leave me fifty dollars note folded in the shape of a *dildo*, otherwise I know where it might end up.

Space permitting.

~~27~~
THAT NIGHT WHEN I WAS SO DRUNK THAT I CAN'T REMEMBER ANYTHING AT ALL

Exactly. So the next chapter is: …

Angry Waiters Federico Fumagalli

~~28~~

DO NOT TOUCH MY ICE CREAM

I always use the stairs to walk down to the Crew Mess from the kitchen that stands one floor up, and today I really want to try a different way: I take the lift.

Big mistake: good habits should die hard.

In the lift I get caught straight away by one of the F&B managers. The same one. There are many of them, but who knows why, I always stumble into the tall and bald Austrian. I'm convinced that he stalks me and follows me and waits for me just for the pleasure of shouting at me whenever I'm doing something that he doesn't like. His uniform is so white and shining that it blinds me. Also, his shoulder straps are decorated in gold. He looks like the superhero of Food & Beverage.

This time he catches me while I'm holding a criminal object: an ice cream. I can't steal ice cream when I am in Donatello dining room (it would be an outrageous ice crime) so I need to ask the Chef.

And that's what I did: I asked the Chef (the same one, the friend of the lobster and the tinfoil). The F&B stops me before I have the chance to press the button 'C' of the lift. He is already inside, ready for the ambush. As he sees me, I can see his lips moving dangerously in a ferocious grin. And in a second I get a shower of angry warnings because I'm not supposed to bring my ice cream to the Crew Mess.

Angry Waiters   *Federico Fumagalli*

He shouts something incomprehensible pointing his finger toward the ice cream, as if he was angry with it. My ice cream is now scared, and wants to melt straight away, but I keep it cool.

The F&B becomes purple-faced and I really can't understand the reason of such anger: I asked permission to the Chef, who himself gave me the ice cream, which is my Holy Grail. The most important thing of the day!

Of my life!

Maybe the F&B is still upset with me because I dared answering back to him on Princess Keys island? Could it be because a few days before I crashed into his sternum while running hard to reach the Teatime?

When he's done with the ronzata, he asks me:

"Do you understand?!"

"Eh?! Were you talking to me?" tough there is no one else in the lift. At this stage he becomes the personification of anger: why should I lose the chance to piss him off a little bit more? I'm already in trouble, why stop here?

He threatens to stick a warning up the dark side of my pelvis if I don't bring the ice cream back, but then he suddenly changes his mind: "Throw it in the bin!"

"WHAAAAT???!!!" I ask, eyes wide open. To me, throwing away an ice cream it's like burning a crucifix of a church, in the church. And then the church.

Ah no, sorry: that would be a pleasure, sorry...

Desperate, because I don't obey, he tries the way of

Angry Waiters   *Federico Fumagalli*

Biblical Superiority: "I am your F&B! You won't have any F&B other than me! Honour your F&B! Don't steal ice creams! Bla, bla, bla..."

He is dismembering my testicles, so I show him that I'm going toward the bin. Instead, once I reach the corner of the kitchen, I run for my life to take the usual staircase for the Crew Mess with the ice cream half melted in my hands, and with a little hope I walk toward the stairs, but...

No.

Surprise of all surprises, somebody is walking up those stairs.

I can't believe it. It's another F&B! The whole F&B army engaged to prevent me from consuming my ice cream! What the hell!

"Let's get it over and done." I murmur myself.

Behind me there's a bin. My ice cream finds its end inside there. I still remember it: chocolate, caramel, vanilla, hazelnuts, wild berries, mint: six flavours I have to say farewell to.

Why? Just tonight that I haven't managed to steal anything from the kitchen (hence, my request for ice cream)!

Upset like God with Sodom and Gomorrah I walk to Canaletto dining room to claim an envelope of tips that wasn't given to me the previous Sunday. The delivery doesn't take place because the one in charge doesn't have the key to the safe, so I doubt that my tips still exist. I give up.

Angry Waiters   *Federico Fumagalli*

In the Crew Mess I can get fragments of half munched food from my Italian colleagues: a spoonful of fruit salad from Roberto, a slice of lasagna from Francesco, half a glass of wine from Flavio.

At midnight I go up to the Crew Bar to buy at least four chocolate bars to placate my hunger and gain some energy, with the intention of accompanying my mouth-watering snacks with a double large pint of Vodka and Cranberry juice.

I'm already eating the third snack when I meet... guess who? That dickhead of an Austrian F&B, already half drunk, who greets and waves "Halllooo!" to me as if I was his best friend ever.

In that exact moment my spoiled mood catches the occasion of a lifetime.

He shouted at me too many times.

He gave me warnings.

He fucked my Agata.

But worst of all: my ice cream.

It's revenge time.

I can easily sacrifice my last Mars bar in favour of this trick. Also, my last Mars bar is starting to melt because of the heat. It's really hot.

I unwrap the Mars bar from its wrapper, and I get close to him from the back. The Crew Bar is really crowded at the moment, we are all stuck together, bodies against bodies. When I'm close enough, with my right hand, light and carefully I slip the Mars bar inside his right back trousers pockets, which are super

Angry Waiters   *Federico Fumagalli*

white and super shining, while at the same time I pick up his mobile phone. It must happen at exactly the same time, to avoid creating an unbalanced movement which generates too much movement later on with the item inside you want to snatch. Something goes inside while something comes out. No other way. His shining trousers are a little bit larger than his size, so I guess they won't make perfect contact with his skin. I don't understand why he keeps his mobile phone in his pocket: in this part of the ocean there is no signal at all, but he is Austrian: maybe his bald head works like an antenna.

My luck is that he is drunker than he seems: he greets *everybody* as he greeted me earlier. I observe him while I walk to sit on one miraculously free armchair around the bar. In my hand stands my trophy.

The F&B sits on a high stool to talk with a girl that much probably won't give herself away to him tonight, but just in case he stood a chance, I already thought of ruining everything.

A quarter of an hour later the heat is unbearable, and the F&B takes his uniform off, remaining just with his white T-shirt showing her two things:

1: his muscles – he should apply for a Men's Health cover

2: how ridiculous he is.

Finally he decides to stand up and order a drink for her. For this, he needs to walk three metres toward the bar.

Angry Waiters   Federico Fumagalli

I watch the girl: her eyes are scanning his unsteady steps, when suddenly she narrows them up to take a closer look to that curious and disgusting brown stain that sprouts from the ass of his white shining trousers.

My Mars bar makes him look like he shat himself.

She looks around; when she is sure that he is not looking at her, she gets off the stool and walks away.

I walk away too.

I need a walk on the deck, just to take in a lungful of fresh air.

Usually, I place myself on the bow to get the feeling of strong wind in my face and look down to the white bright foam of the sea against the ship. Then I look up to the sky.

I hope this is not forbidden.

After a while I move to the starboard side, on the right, where it is usually very dark. Not completely, but almost. I pull out his phone from my pocket: it's grey, very small, no antennas; the display has a nice blue colour. It could be a cool one, if only I could see a signal of some sort, but on the blue display appears 'No Service'.

My face displays an evil grin; my fingers work for a while, trying to enter in the Text Messages menu. When I find it (quite difficultly; everything is written in Austrian), I write inside: *'You are gonna die in 10, 9, 8, 7, 6...!'* and with a pleasure of vengeance I let the phone depart for its destiny, sinking into the unknown.

My dear F&B: with one move I deprived you of sex

~233~

with that chick in the bar, and I deprived you of your 'cool' mobile.

Do you still want to stick a warning up the dark side of my pelvis?

Next time, let me eat my ice cream.

~~29~~
THE CONQUEST OF SAINT MARTIN

Oh, come on… I never have a day off, which is equal to the six hours on Saturday if I am not involved in some painful duty, and then when it should be possible to get off at Saint Martin I have to waste time for the Bow Drill…

So: maybe I am on two weeks of Dining Room Shift, and if one week I'm working in Saint Martin, I will be off in Saint Thomas. Next week would be the opposite. I prefer Saint Martin to Saint Thomas, and this week I am *off* in Saint Martin. Great! I could go to the beach and ride a jet ski!

I could…

No! I can't!

There's this bloody Bow Drill, which nobody has ever understood what kind of utility it might have, other than wasting time.

It should be a general exercise for emergencies, where each one should demonstrate to be able to do his job safely. And I don't want to discuss it: it could be really useful, *if only we really made it!* But…

Just before we finish serving breakfast, or right after, the general alarm goes off. As soon as I hear it, no matter what I'm doing, I must run to my cabin and wear my life jacket, a hat and collect my Blue card. Even if I was serving tea and coffee to my Passengers, it doesn't matter: stop it and run! I leave them to their useless destiny and I start the Drill.

When I am dressed up like a 'Saviour of Souls On board' I walk calmly toward my Muster Station, somewhere upstairs, I give my code to the pretty Supervisor, I imagine her naked, she imagines me dead, and I go to sit down together with somebody that usually doesn't talk too much. Someone who talks too much always generates attention by a third party, taking with him the innocent ones like me that has no desire of answering unwanted questions. Indeed: sometimes the Supervisor asks some questions, and sometimes somebody is even able to answer correctly. Not too often, but it happens. The Supervisor must ensure and confirm our poor level of preparation: it's just a matter of a few random questions, followed by random answers. Once I even gave out a correct explanation about the usage of the fire breaking doors, and that's only because on my first induction I answered correctly to the same question. If the ship is sinking, I'm the man ~~who makes it sink.~~

But for example, how many people could stand on the emergency life boat? Between forty and fifty, but for me it would sink with only fifteen of these overweight Passengers.

This drill, unfortunately, doesn't take place often. Most of the times there is nothing happening. Nothing of nothing. Sometimes, there is not even somebody: nobody to say anything about doing nothing. The emptiness at our total disposition. We sit down for one

Angry Waiters   *Federico Fumagalli*

hour, slowly starting to fall asleep with our life jackets on (from the window we can be seen by worried Passengers), or quietly beginning to swear in thirty languages, thinking about missing the chance of being on solid ground.

If I am lucky (almost never), the speakers spark up announcing that the Bow Drill has come to an end, and we can all go to hell.

Ended? It hasn't even started!

Instead, if I am unlucky (all the other times), I am transferred with the herd of work*mates* to another ballroom; sometimes it's the theatre, sometimes it's the Donatello dining room, where guests have been left alone ever since and they are asked to move out. Here too, the waiting is useless and very long, and when everybody has lost patience, and bad words have the upper hand, the speakers spark up announcing that the Bow Drill has come to an end, and we can all go to hell.

Very nice.

But when there is no Bow Drill whatsoever to smash my balls: green light! Go! Go! GOOO!! Away from this ship! I want to feel firm ground! I want to stand without rolling!

I get off the ship from the bow or midship, I insert my Laminex in the machine, I wait to hear BLIP-BLOP, I rush with my claws open to grab the mooring – like the vulture on the shrew – I raise my head and I burp from happiness.

Angry Waiters   *Federico Fumagalli*

I want to go down town, and I have two choices: taxi boat, or normal taxi. My option is the taxi with wheels, on firm road, for three US dollars. I open the door and I take in the wonderful heat of the Caribbean. Walking up and down the streets I can spot hundreds of jewellery shops. They are of no interest to me: what are of interest to me are the beauties in bikinis.

First of all I need lunch: I find a healthy fast food, where a milkshake is thought for people of a certain size (I could survive three days with one of those), and the fried chicken is not cut into pieces: the chicken is fried still alive, the whole piece except the feathers, inside the monthly changed frying oil. They also give you chicken's feet for free.

After the light meal I lay on the beach, spreading out my giant beach towel with dolphin print, finally relaxing on the sand. The heat is really burning me, and of course I forgot the sunscreen. I think that it's not too bad to try my luck for just a couple of hours…

After ten minutes I really need a drink. My milkshake is evaporated, I can also hear the chicken shouting 'I'm thirsty!' from inside my stomach, so I walk to the bar *'P-irate of the Caribbean'*, decorated with a giant P-irate, very thirsty and of course very pissed off. On his left black eyepatch someone has painted a pint of beer.

Since I'm not a beer drinker, under thirty-five degrees and two hours to kill before duty, I order a double Pina Colada that the barman gives me with two straws: one for me and one for the huge chicken in my belly.

I might look pregnant, but I swear I'm not.

I fall asleep deeply for the luxury of twenty minutes, when I suddenly wake up thanks to a water balloon that my work*mates* have thrown at me. Their intention is to rent a few Jet Skis, and my comment is: *'OK, stronzi: adesso vi faccio un culo così!'* – OK, you morons, now I kick your ass!

We go to the rental desk, but I realise that I'm not in the condition to drive a Jet Ski. My head is spinning, alcohol is having fun in my blood, my vision blurs.

But it doesn't matter! Fuck it! Come on! Give me a Jet Ski! You'll all drink my piss! Go! Go! Go!

Unfortunately, the danger of reciprocal collision is too high, and after twenty minutes the lifeguards on the beach call us back. We seem to be too dangerous for the bathers in the sea, and for the dolphins. End of the fun.

After a glass of water to wash away the sand from my mouth, I gain back my mental powers, but even with this faculty fully working, I don't manage to understand that doing business abroad is not always convenient, especially in the electronic gadget field.

The first error I make is the purchase of a small mobile phone as a gift for my dad: this island is under the French-Dutch dominion, and the mobile turns out to be useless.

I enter a mobile phone shop because in the outside showcase I spot a cute and small mobile, not so

Angry Waiters   *Federico Fumagalli*

expensive. About two hundred US dollars. I ask the man at the counter if I can try it: I insert my Italian Vodafone SIM Card and the phone works perfectly. I call my friend, explore the menu... Excellent! It's mine.

I put the SIM Card back in my old Panasonic GD90 pineapple size and I make sure that he gives me exactly the phone that I tried, not a similar one from another box. I can see it from the beginning, so when it comes to me I am sure that I'm purchasing a perfectly working phone as a gift for my dad.

And that's how they fuck me. Once I've gone away (and this is the last time I will ever come to Saint Martin), I discover that my new phone can only work with the SIM Card I first used to try it, my Italian SIM Card. Its code is locked and it doesn't matter how many PIN or PUK codes I put: the phone is self-locked. Forever.

Weeks before, on this island, I bought one of the things I'm most proud of having: a massive stereo.

A massive stereo with two speakers, with two hundred watts output and three other little speakers for any kind of effect: Surround, Home Theatre, and whatsoever. What is needed to be mentioned is the capacity of storing inside sixty CDs: the compartment is like a round tube carousel with sixty little hooks on the lower side; the CDs have to be put inside in vertical position side by side. For me, it's the best stereo I have ever seen. I don't even need to stand up from my bed

Angry Waiters   *Federico Fumagalli*

to change CD: they're all inside.

I can also set the alarm to wake up in the morning with the music I want, and this makes me hyper-happy. I can also fight with the bass sound of the stereo of the Mexican guy on the other side of the wall, first because my speakers are much more powerful, and then because I don't listen to reggae or hip hop or other annoying music: in my stereo there's only Heavy Metal. Want to challenge me with a couple of songs of Children of Bodom at 03.00 at night?

The price of this mammoth is three hundred and seventy-five US dollars, but with my attention to detail I can rebate the price to three hundred dollars. If they can afford to lower the price by seventy-five dollars, it means that they still make a good profit out of it, so I guess the real price could be around two hundred dollars, no more.

The problem is the transport: 'How the hell do I bring it back to my cabin?' I say to myself after I pay. The packaging is so large I could hide inside.

I can't even rely on my Italian friend who left me alone with it. I recruit a mercenary salesman and his trolley to give me a hand to the taxi boat, but then, I'm alone again. I can't lift it.

My luck has the name of Robert and Peter, two polish workmates who give me a hand to bring it to my cabin, drops of sweat on our foreheads.

My only friends here come from Poland, the

Angry Waiters   *Federico Fumagalli*

Philippines and Thailand. Just two from Italy, one from Slovakia.

The afternoon of pleasure ends up, no more Saint Martin for me; I go back in my dog house for a quick shower and get ready for another dinner. Also, tonight there is another Galley Round: tomorrow we stop in Saint Thomas, US Territory, there's the USPH danger. To finish, as usual, I wish *dobranoc* to my room-mate Robert and I fall asleep, exhausted.

Angry Waiters   *Federico Fumagalli*

~~30~~
SAINT THOMAS

I'm facing one of the tall glass windows on the Horizon Court together with Ramil, my best workmate from the Philippines, and I have almost finished *sanitising* after breakfast. The line where I'm working has been closed earlier because all Passengers are gone already; at 10.00 they are down on the island, in this splendid day of super-shining sun. This means that one line only is required to fix the remaining Passengers' stomachs.

Ramil is a very nice guy, always happy and smiling and with something funny and clever to say – the total opposite of me. How does he do it? I don't know. I mean: being so happy at any time of the day, even when on duty the shit hits the fan, is something I can't manage. But I like being with him because he puts me in good mood, which is difficult.

Soon we'll finish our Lido Breakfast shift and we can get off to have some fun with *them*.

Them… Who?

Well... them!

In front of us there is the giant Disney Cruise Ship: as I said, we are in front of the glass window, and we are trying to communicate with gestures and signs with two young and very attractive Chinese girls who are doing the same job as us at their own buffet on the Disney Ship. We are trying to understand at what time they will be finishing, so that we can meet them and go

~243~

Angry Waiters   *Federico Fumagalli*

together somewhere.

Our attempt fails miserably when the Head Waiter Mickey Mouse on their ship catches them flirting with staff of a rival cruise, and they are forced to leave the buffet.

We look at each other, giving up, then suddenly explode in laughter for five long, long seconds, until our Head Waiter Donald ~~Fuck~~ Duck taps his hands on our shoulders.

Time's up: shift ends and we run the hell out of here. Since we can't meet the Chinese girls, Ramil prefers to sleep one hour; we split and I go to get changed and rush out as impetuously as a tsunami ready to smash his espresso-like free time. Better say that I feel powerful like a little wave moved by a teaspoon in the coffee cup.

Before I can jump off the ship, I insert my Laminex in the machine, wait for its BLIP-BLOP, and a wave of heat hits me: outside it is thirty-six degrees, while inside the ship the air conditioning is set at around sixteen degrees.

Thirty-six degrees is exactly what I need.

In Saint Thomas I don't really have to take the taxi to go down town, there's enough stuff in the near surroundings.

With all the things that I could do on a Caribbean island, when it's thirty-six degrees, at 11.30am, the first thing I do is walk into a takeaway pizzeria and I order one Margherita. And thank God, they have

Angry Waiters   *Federico Fumagalli*

Fanta, the excellence of all beverages.

After lunch I jump to an internet point, I check my e-mails, and I call home to notify that I'm still alive. There must be something wrong with phone companies: I don't understand how come if I call Italy from the Caribbean with a Calling Card, I spend less than calling Italy from Italy with a mobile phone. WTH...?

Then I meet Luca, a good workmate and friend: he's going down town to have lunch in a place that he describes as 'pretty yummy'. We get on the free bus that travels on the opposite side of the road.

"Where's everyone else? I haven't seen anyone around." I ask him.

"They've gone to church."

"*Where* have they gone?!"

"To church!" He repeats.

"What for?" I ask, as I've never thought that any of us would be so dumb to waste their free time in a church. "And by the way: a church in the Caribbean? I thought the only religion here was *Bob-Marleyism*! Believers sing 'No woman no cry', 'The Virgin Mary-juana'... They smoke the Holy Spirit!"

"Fede, are you kidding me? They went to... church! You know, the church... Church! That other kind of church..." he says, embarrassed.

"... Mosque?"

"... What the fuck you saying... Really you don't know?"

Angry Waiters *Federico Fumagalli*

"Nope."

"Let's say that it's a kind of church where the various Marys are not entirely virgin; and in the confessional, sins are not listened to and forgiven: they are committed; and they are the ones to take your *host* in their mouth..."

"OK, OK! I got it!" I stop him. "It's a brothel!"

"Well done! You are not completely retarded after all!" He laughs at me.

"And... how much is... the offer?"

"It depends on which *prayer* you want: fifty dollars for the *Lord's Prayer*, seventy-five dollars for the *Holy Mary*. Don't know about the whole *Sermon* but I can ask around."

"A bit expensive, eh?"

"If you want something cheaper, next week they're going to the Buddhist Temple."

"WTH is that? But anyway I'm quite scared of Buddha size ladies."

"It could be interesting. They cost less, and there's a fruit basket with three bananas included in the price."

"What the fuck are those for?!"

"Well, I guess the remaining one is for you to eat, hahaha!"

"Jesus Christ! Now I understand why everyone comes to me to pay them to do my Teatime duty, Napkin Folding, etc...!"

"Exactly! You are paying for their whores!"

"Bloody bastards! I pay them to do my job, I can't

Angry Waiters   *Federico Fumagalli*

sleep anyway, and they use my money to fuck like pigs! I'm so pissed off!" I complain.

"You are a celebrity among Junior Waiters!" he keeps laughing at me.

"I hate everybody."

"And they have also fucked Agata, the only money free bitch in the Caribbean, hahaha!"

I hate the whole world.

The bus stops and we sit in this restaurant of which I forgot the name, and we order the compulsory alcoholic drinks (compulsory for us, not for the restaurant).

After that, the waiter hands us the menus. I look through the hole that mine has on top of the page, scanning the view outside: ships and yachts are moored forty meters away. The beach is on our left, filled up with beauties I'll never manage to get to. Sun is burning down. And flies are flying around.

Coming to the menu, I order pasta that as per the menu should be: 'Penne pasta with Giant, Enormous, Massive, Fearsome prawns, with broccoli', that I ask without broccoli.

"Certainly!" is the waiter's answer, and he keeps his word: after twenty-five minutes I get my pasta without broccoli but... *with cheese*. I look at it, disgusted: "Why did they put cheese, if there is fish? I hate cheese. There's nothing else I hate more than cheese!" I complain with Luca. In Italy, you *never* mix cheese

Angry Waiters   *Federico Fumagalli*

with fish, not even on pasta.

Never mind: I take out the cheese with the straw of my Double Strawberry Daiquiri, and then I try to check the prawns that should have been pillow size, instead I can hardly pick them up with the fork. They are so small they fall between the prongs. To eat them, I need to squeeze my brain to find some sort of trick.

After my second lunch, we take a walk among the open market on the street, looking at the women and giving them marks and prices depending on what they are wearing. Grown up men's talk, there it is.

I feel my Double Strawberry Daiquiri playing inside me... my head is dizzy...

Both me and Luca come back to the ship by taxi, sleep an hour, and then start again: shower, uniform, duty, fatigue, fake smiles, maybe a dinner...

... and a quick prayer in the bathroom...

~~31~~
SALARY ON THE SEABED

A round of applause for the Accounting department: as soon as I have the chance to save some money they lose them straight away. A team of real hopeless employees.

On the 3rd of March, I follow the suggestion of my colleagues and I send some money home, because if I come back home with more than ten thousand US dollars in cash (I wish I could) I should declare it to customs.

I grab my little envelope with my two thousand dollars, which seems a lot, but it's just twenty miserable little hundred dollar notes, and I walk on toward the Crew Office with the intention to transfer my money to my Italian bank account. Another reason is the problem of theft: since I can't trust anybody, except for my two Polish friends Robert M. and S., I don't want to keep too much money in my room. I can't even trust my cleaner boy: one day seven pairs of my socks simply disappeared. Vanished. Usually I wash them in the micro-sink, but those days I bought more of them just to avoid washing them too often and save time. One time I had a lot of them I put them inside a plastic bag and left them to him.

The socks seemed not to be returning any more. To get them back, I had to threaten Mr Cleaner (Arlan) with not paying any more bills and no more tips. As for

Angry Waiters   Federico Fumagalli

magic, my socks reappeared: clean, dried, ironed, folded and perfumed. I don't even know who Arlan is, I never see his face, I just know that he comes in my room to clean when I'm sweating in the dining room.

Anyway, when I arrive to the Crew Office I give the fat lady my international bank details, I sign thousands of papers and I hand her my hard-earned two thousand dollars.

"It will take about two weeks." She tells me.

"Two weeks? How does it get there, on a kayak?"

One month has gone, and my bank manager says that my money has not arrived.

I confirm that my codes are correct and I come back to the Crew Office to check them again: they are indeed correct, the bank is correct, my money has run away. It escaped without me.

This little detail upsets me one hundred on a scale of one to ten, but the fat lady tells me to come back one week later.

One week later: I am more disappointed than one week earlier. The money is gone without saying 'goodbye'. But where? On the ship it is not, and in the bank it hasn't arrived. Did it sink?

The chubby lady behind the desk, really concerned about my problem, tells me: "Sorry, it happens sometimes." As if this were enough to placate my devastating wrath.

One thousand three hundred ~~shrew~~ crew members,

~250~

Angry Waiters   *Federico Fumagalli*

am I the only lemon to which this had to happen?

Rumours tell about the legend of another proud crew member to whom the Crew Office had lost his eight thousand dollars.

On his disembarking day, his money still hadn't reappeared. For revenge, he didn't get off the ship. He remained on board hiding and sleeping for a few days anywhere possible, dressed like a normal person and eating for free.

After a few days they realised he was on board using facilities that were prohibited to him when on duty, and as by magic the Crew Office found his money and gave it back to him. Money came from nowhere, but he took it without complaining, he picked up his luggage, and got off the ship on the same day.

I decide to try the same thing, in case this would happen to me.

I come back to the Crew Office after another week, furious. I don't tell them about my intention, but I make my point very clear: no money, no Federico off the ship. I inform the Maître d' about the situation and I wait, carrying on working like a donkey with a ☹ on my face.

A few days before my disembarkation I get a call from the Crew Office. Maybe they smelled the danger of having me on board in a bad mood, but at the desk the fat lady announces to me proudly: "Mr Frutteric! Here you go: your two thousand dollars! Happy now? We've found them!"

"No! You stripeless zebra! It should be in my bank account!"

I stare at her: she is giving me back the same little envelope containing the same twenty notes I gave her ages before! My money has always been in their safe! It has never been touched!

"Anything else I can do for you, Mr Frutteric?"

I ☺ back to her: "Please, no!" I say leaving the office. "Just: do not procreate."

~~32~~
MISSION IMPUSSYBLE

She is the one who first nods to me about moving to a quieter place, away from the crowd.

Like lightning we cross the corridor and we call the lift. While we wait for it to come up to the Crew Bar on Deck 8, she grabs my arm with her hands and gets closer to me, munching my earlobe. After, she gulps down a few drops of my Vodka and Cranberry juice, inserting the straw between her lips with such sensuality that the lemon slice in the cocktail dries up straight away.

The lift arrives, and out of it come Raszvan and my room-mate Robert.

Which means…

Which means…

MY CABIN IS FREE!

Without losing grip of my arm she drags me inside the lift. With my free arm I press the button for Deck 4: while descending she starts kissing me; with one hand she's still grabbing my arm, and with her other hand she grabs… my other hand that's holding the big glass of Vodka and Cranberry juice: does she want to kiss me, or to suck my ~~cock~~...tail, or what?

In a blink of an eye the lift door opens up, there's no one around:

"*On This Way!*" I declare, and in another blink of an eye we are in front of my cabin.

Angry Waiters   *Federico Fumagalli*

Looking for my Key Card is not easy, I'm so excited – as much as she is-; in the meanwhile, still in the corridor, she warms herself by sucking with greed and pleasure... *my drink*. She has almost finished it, and I'm a little disappointed because since I bought it I hadn't had the chance to drink it.

But actually it doesn't matter too much: I'm very close to get very intimate with this beautiful Polish girl, and tomorrow first thing first I'll ~~steal~~ buy a bottle of champagne. No, she is not Agata: to hell with Agata!

I finally find my wallet, containing hundreds of cards: I deal all of them in the hope to get the right one – 3329 – to open the door and consume this miracle called 'Night of *Prayers*'. The whole sermon for free!

But... what the hell...! She is dropping all *my drink* on the neckline of her dress, under which I can't get a glimpse of any bra at all. I raise my eyes to the ceiling – a little bit in delight, a little bit because she could have asked me if I wanted some of *my drink* before covering her tits with it.

I find my key card, hands shaking, I kick the door open, and before I can invite her in – she's already inside. I throw the empty glass to the end of the corridor, I close the door with four locks, I switch on the stereo with a CD of ballads and I observe this splendid girl: long dark waving hair touching her back, clear bright eyes, few freckles on her face.

I can see my big ☺☺☺ reflected in her mirroring eyes. There are not too many words between us, but we

Angry Waiters   *Federico Fumagalli*

both know what to do.

She grabs my head leaning it onto her breast, where I finally take the situation under control and I lower the shoulder straps of her dress. I make it fall down to her waist, and I confirm my doubt: she isn't wearing any bra at all, and I remain with her heaving boobs in my hands, boobs that still smell of *my* Vodka and Cranberry juice. Not thinking too much, I do everything possible to reclaim my drink back till the last drop; they are great anti-stress toys: you squeeze them and it's good for your health.

I see that she likes it, she laughs, she plays, so I go down a little bit without taking my tongue off her skin. I get down to her belly button, I stop and raise my eyes to ask for directions: "On this way!" she says, showing me the exact location with a finger.

My cock is barking at the moon, even though it's still inside my combat uniform.

She notices my moment of hesitation, she gives me knowing eyes, and I can't wait any more: I pull away her skirt. Hey Austrian F&B! Come and stop me now!

I finish slowly what I'm doing, before changing subject and starting the real thing, but suddenly I hear a strange noise... a noise that shouldn't be there...

...Suddenly I realise that I no longer have my watch on my wrist...

...an alarm rings inside me...

...my vision is a blur...

...the Polish girl is vanishing away from my sight...

Angry Waiters   *Federico Fumagalli*

…and from my touch…

…and from my tongue…

I lay alone in my bed, with the clock blipping on the little shelf behind my head; its annoying sound is like an earthquake in my mind; I wake up really, really, really upset, like a cheetah deprived of its prey, because… Why is it every time I'm dreaming girls I have to wake up?! Why?! ☹

However, it felt somehow real.

I open the curtain which separates my bed from the centimetric-wide room and I rush in the bathroom: my cock is furious, as if somebody was playing *tug of war*, and I perform a free *Holy Mary*.

After the cold shower I walk on duty to listen to the Supervisor who is making the roll call; on the way I notice a broken glass at the end of the corridor: it's the one I threw away a few hours earlier.

At the meeting I count the female work*mates*: one of them is missing.

When she finally arrives, my face becomes pale.

I'm quite surprised: it's Aneta. She is never late.

Dreams that feel real, forgotten broken glasses and a never-late girl who comes late: coincidence? Effect of hangover?

A doubt assaults me: how many Vodka and Cranberry juice did I drink? Maybe I was too drunk and we really had sex? Or maybe we didn't have sex

~256~

Angry Waiters   *Federico Fumagalli*

because we were too drunk?

But... no! *She* drank all *my drink*!

Besides, if I wasn't drunk, why would I throw a glass in the corridor?

My stomach's burning... I need to know: have we done it or not?

I observe her, waiting to meet her eyes; I need to spot some light at the end of the tunnel. Her eyes are bright as if she's stayed awake the whole night and drank a few drinks... but... I'm a bit confused. I concentrate on her, but she catches me while I'm almost dribbling. I drop the maniac look off my face: "What's wrong with you?" she asks me.

"No, nothing! A bit sleepy... how about you? Good sleep?" I reply.

"Not really." She says yawning big time. "I'm feeling wrecked."

"Why is that?" I ask, as if nothing is going on in my mind.

"I think I drank too much... but at least I had fun..." and she blinks and ☺s.

There you go! So something must have happened! The thing is that with those words she confuses me much more. It's obvious that she doesn't come and tell me how nice it was fucking with me, maybe she is as confused as I am, and maybe she is throwing out few words just to see how I react. And unfortunately I'm not good at all in these matters.

"And what did you do last night?" she wants to know.

Angry Waiters   *Federico Fumagalli*

But why would she ask?

What could I answer?

Nothing at all, the Supervisor is giving out orders and duties: Aneta is at the Box; I am Cleaning Tables, and so I have the chance to go back and forth from the tables to her station with heaps of dirty plates.

Each time I get close, I ☺; she does too.

Even in the rare moments when I have little to do, I fool around her; I need to find the right moment to attack her on the emotional front: I absolutely want to find out what happened last night, if something happened.

Maybe she is faking her interest just to see what the hell I am doing; maybe she wants to see if I make an effort to tell her straight, but I would never have the braveness of such a thing.

Or maybe nothing happened and she is probably thinking that this morning I'm just a little bit more deficient than usual.

When I reappear in front of her she gives me sweet eyes and she asks me if I can cover her while she eats a couple of pastries she has stolen from the fridge. I reply that I would cover her even if she wasn't eating, then she gets down behind the box to accomplish this illegal action called *eating on duty*, with me standing up outside keeping an eye on incoming Supervisors.

Once finished she stands up and she licks her fingers with such sexy moves that even the quiet sea becomes rough; she tells me that inside the box, if I turn around,

Angry Waiters   *Federico Fumagalli*

there is something sweet for me. Fantasies get back to me, but soon I come back to reality: I have been caught enough times eating on duty, but she can cover me and I am safe. But then... where's the problem? I'm leaving soon!

I take her place, kneeling down, well hidden, I open the little door and I find a Fruit Tartlet and a Gianduia's Bigne. Two of my favourites pastries.

"I know you like them!" she says.

Great! She remembered it! And she stole them for me! Maybe...

"Thanks! You are a girl to marry!" I whisper.

"I know! I wouldn't mind to settle down."

"But... don't you have a boyfriend?"

"Of course not, up here it's almost impossible to have a stable relationship. Besides, if you look for a relationship with somebody on ground, you are finished. You better find somebody on board, or don't even apply for this job. Otherwise you do like most people do and you get off with anyone who needs sex. Or you should be *gay*. Are you gay?"

"... Me?!?"

I wonder why everybody ask me if I'm gay.

"How about you, did you ever get off with someone here, just for... fun?"

She doesn't even blink. She strikes me with her eyes wide open:

"No! Never! I'm *not* that kind of girl! Come on! I'm not Agata!"

~259~

Angry Waiters   *Federico Fumagalli*

"Of course not, yeah, right… it's exactly what I thought you'd say…" I sadly reply.

The mystery is sorted out. It couldn't be any worse.

Or could it?

On my way back to another box I wish I could hit Passengers with a nunchaku. For their safety I decide to pass through the kitchen and swear loudly against the world and the Gods.

Then I hear something that sounds like my name.

"Fredrico! There you go! I was just looking for you!"

It can't be a God.

No: another Head Waiter, another name spelled wrongly.

"Me? What for?"

"First of all, how are you?" he asks me.

"As usual, it's the worst day of my cruise."

"The worst day of your cruise *until now!*"

"?" I reply.

"Do you know anything at all about a mysterious Mars bar, a missing mobile phone, a broken glass, a roll of tinfoil…?"

"No, nothing at all. Why?" I lie, while my heart stops beating.

"Then, if you don't know anything at all, you should come with me to the Maître d' office *again*, and everything will be clear. We'll show you how CCTV cameras work on this ship." He ☺s at me.

Great. Not exactly the happy ending I was wishing for.

~260~

Back in the Maître d' office, which now starts to feel like home, I'm sitting on a soft and comfortable chair with the Head Waiter, looking at a variety of screens: on one of them there is some footage running in which I worryingly recognise myself.

"Do you recognise yourself, Mr Fumagayli?" He asks me.

"Uhm... No." I reply.

"Are you sure? That's clearly you. Don't you think so?"

I look straight at the screen, undecided to either lie or confess.

"Uhm... Well... I can't see properly... He doesn't really look like me."

"Mr Fumagayli, look at this footage carefully: are you telling me that the person who is inserting a Mars bar in the ass of that F&B Manager is *not* you?"

The CCTV has recorded the moment when I was taking revenge on the bald Austrian.

"Uhm... the image is not so clear. I can't really say..."

"Fumagayli! The image is so clear that I can read 'Mars' on the wrapping paper. Don't try to fool me. Now look at what happens in a few moments."

I know already what happens in a few moments. Still undecided about lying or confessing.

The video shows my hands taking something out of the Austrian's pockets.

"Are these your hands?" He asks me, pointing at the

screen.

"Well... they could be anyone's hands... and there is lot of people around... I can't really say..."

"If you can't really say, look at the next footage."

I also know what happens in the next footage: me holding a mobile phone, just before I throw it at sea.

"Look, Fumagayli."

"*If you don't stop calling me Fumagayli, I rip your face off.*"

He carries on: "Here the same person that looks so much like you is playing with a phone which presumably is the same one that was in the pockets of your best friend. Am I right?"

I make a doubtful face: "Actually, it's very dark outside... It's hard to say. You can't be sure it's me, although I agree he looks so much like me; and the phone, you have already said *presumably*, which says a lot..."

He covers his face with both hands. "Fumagayli, do you have a justification for everything?"

"Actually, could you *not* call me *Fumagayli*? It's getting on my nerves."

"OK, Frederico..."

I raise my eyes to the sky. If it wasn't for all these CCTV cameras in the room...

"So," he carries on, "Let's skip to the next footage: do you recognise this corridor?"

Of course I recognise it: it's the one where my cabin is.

Angry Waiters   *Federico Fumagalli*

"Uhm... No. All those corridors look the same to me..."

"Is your cabin number 3329?"

"Yes it is." I can't lie to this one.

"And... don't you see the number on the door from this camera?"

"Uhm... well... the image is too bright..."

"Oh come on! Before it was too dark, now it's too bright! It is 3329, it's there, nice and clear, you can't deny it."

"OK then, I won't deny it."

I can see he's just about to explode.

"Now look at the guy walking towards the door: what is he holding?"

It's undeniable: that's me, holding a glass. I can even see there's a Vodka and Cranberry juice inside.

"Uhm... it looks like a glass..." I confess.

"Very good. Finally you say something right. Now tell me: is that you, Frederico?"

My heart stops. Not only is 200% obvious that it's me, but I must have been too drunk to remember what is happening. I am walking with no balance whatsoever, bouncing left and right, apparently laughing out loud – although, thank god, there is no audio – until I reach my door and I struggle to open it. I can't insert my key card because my hands are shaking, and then I suddenly get rid of my cocktail throwing it away. It shatters into pieces on the stairs nearby.

Angry Waiters   *Federico Fumagalli*

"Frederico? Anything to say?"

"Can I have a lawyer?"

"No, you don't deserve one. Now look at what happens: I wouldn't be too proud of myself if that happened to me."

What? As far as I remember (besides thinking that I was with Aneta), after that I entered my cabin.

But... no. If I hadn't seen the video myself, I would not have believed it.

For no reason whatsoever, with my hands I hold the sides of the door and bend my legs slightly, then I move my crotch back and forth as if I was fucking the door.

Yep: embarrassed like never before, I am watching myself while *sexually assaulting* the door of my cabin.

"So, tell me Frederico: is that *you*, groping the door before finally getting inside properly? And I mean: inside of your cabin."

My face is red and I am burning. It is obvious that it's me.

"Uhm... I don't remember doing this..."

"It doesn't matter what you remember. But you do agree that it is *you*, right?"

"It could be my cabin mate, Robert M."

"Robert is three metres taller than you! Come on, Fumagayli: just say it was you! That guy is *you!*"

"Which guy?" I ask nonchalantly: "I don't see anyone."

As a matter of fact, in the video I am now inside my

Angry Waiters *Federico Fumagalli*

cabin: all you can see is the shattered glass on the floor of the corridor.

The Head Waiter loses his patience. He has had enough of me.

"Frederico, you have just wasted half an hour of my life. I will pretend nothing happened, but now please disappear from me and don't do anything stupid any more: If you do, I shall inform your Austrian friend. And if this happens..."

"...The dark side of my pelvis will be in danger?"

"Exactly. Now go, I don't want to see you any more!"

It's said that cruise ships are a paradise for the ones looking for lot of sex: it's true (not for me, of course), especially for gay people. There are hundreds of good looking girls, the kind you would take for one-night stand, but there is also a high concentration of Men who like other Men, which worries me because I can't understand why, but Men are attracted to me. Women don't give a damn, but Men do. It's not like I'm so handsome and irresistible; I wouldn't even pose on a Men's Health cover.

I receive weekly indecent proposals from guys of all age and ranks, all of them politely but quickly declined in virtue of my strong preference toward the other sex.

I never have problems about insistent people, because they just don't care: if it's not me, it will be someone else.

Some of the questions I am often asked are:

Angry Waiters   *Federico Fumagalli*

"Do you have a girlfriend?"

"No."

"Do you have a boyfriend?"

"No!"

"So why did you get on board, if you're going to get your ass s-*crew-ed* anyway?"

Good question.

The last Waiter I work with is gay. Portuguese, he is – I admit – a rather handsome guy: honest, happy, and one of the best employees. He had always wanted to work with me (surely not for my abilities), but never had the chance.

One day I am forced to change Waiter again, because of our 'incompatibility of characters', and this guy, Baptista, comes to ask me if I wouldn't mind being his Junior Waiter. For me it is OK, I say yes, but from that day I wear a chastity belt. Preventing is much better than curing.

We start working in Bernini dining room: this is very good news, after three weeks in Donatello, now I have to fight with less work*mates*. Or less work*mates* who have to fight with me.

On our first ~~date~~ day, Baptista wants to make things clear: "For each mistake you make, your ass is mine."

Great.

Since I'm going to face harder times, I enter the dining room with a perfectionist mindset: mistakes – of which I am a master – will have to be kept at a mini minimum.

While I finish duty with Baptista, I find out that my friend Sayapong – a very short Thai guy who looks twenty, but he is thirty – has a secret to reveal to me: he is in love with me.

"I'm sorry Pingpong: you are a good guy, but no: thanks for the offer, I'm not interested." I explain.

"Why, do you have another boyfriend?" he asks me.

"Why isn't the question: do you have a girlfriend?"

"Well… Yes! I'm sorry…" It's all I can say, big dickhead that I am.

"Oh, I see. But why not me?" he asks disappointed.

Good question. Why not him?

"Because…" I try to think of something. "I like tall guys…?"

And in that moment I feel a wall of shame crumbling onto me. Why did I say that?!? I did not need to lie to him.

I start counting the *minutes* remaining to my disembarkation.

~~33~~
FORT LAUDERDALE AND MIAMI
(Wake up, lazy motherfucker!)

If my superiors haven't scheduled me for some surprise duty, on Saturday I can get off on solid ground at Port Everglades, which is the name of the port in Fort Lauderdale.

This morning's surprise is that the bad luck caught somebody else: an FBI team came on board to check a Suspicious Boy guilty of drugs possession in his cabin. He is one of the Crew, of course, and this is something that the Management wants to try to hide from the Passengers with every possible effort. This makes me laugh: how can you hide something like this, when even sniffer dogs were barking at everything? Armed police, a guy in his breakfast uniform exiting from the gangway with handcuffs on... How the hell can they hide this from the Passengers that are always around? They are human beings, and they will surely ask us "What happened to that guy?"

"Which guy? I know nothing." We should answer.

But I don't give a damn about drugs and dogs and guys and curious Passengers: I just want to hold onto my hardly earned six hours off!

I put my Laminex in the machine, I wait for the usual BLIP-BLOP, and I exit to inhale the summer heat. I walk to the calling centre for an hour of internet and calls, after that I sit in Angelo's Pizza; here the pizza is pretty good and tasty.

By chance I meet Luca again, with whom I went downtown with in Saint Thomas, and we find a bar for a round of Margaritas to consecrate the universal toast:

"Brindiamo a una cosa che finisce per *No!*" he says. "Alla figa, *No?*"

(Let's cheers to that one thing that ends with *No!* … To pussy, *No?*"

Straight after we decide to go and do some damage in Miami: we hire a taxi and we get taxied into this big city. It costs us seventy-five dollars.

"Damn you, for seventy-five dollars I could have had a Holy Mary." he complains to me about the driver.

We pay, we exit the car park, and we make our appearance in a giant shopping centre fooling around in the shops, especially the shop with both male and female underwear. We stay in between the two, keeping an eye on every girl, commenting on them, and asking useless questions to the cute saleswomen about hypothetical sexy items as gifts for our hypothetical girlfriends (or boyfriends).

Half an hour later, the saleswoman has had enough of the two of us; we understand she might call security, so we get out avoiding Sexual Harassment's charges for our malicious eyes.

Heading for a fast food buffet we gulp down some food, without realising the unbelievable price and the unbelievable portion we have been given: too high the

Angry Waiters   *Federico Fumagalli*

first, too little the second.

Straight after that follows the real deal of the day: we are in a chocolate shop, Godiva, where for a diamond's price we can have any kind of chocolate in any form, shape, taste and colour. Everything is made with chocolate, so that we are tempted to lick the sugary lady behind the dark chocolate counter, just to see if she melts in our mouths.

There's chocolate in a Lasagna shape, a Lamborghini, Santa Claus, books, shelves with dwarfs where even the shelves are made of chocolate, watches, sunglasses… everything. What we don't find is a chocolate vagina; as an alternative there is a huge dark chocolate penis which makes us feel hopeless and miserable.

We make our choice, we pay with gold because our cash seems not to be enough, and then unconsciously we enter a shop that sells everything that works with a plug or batteries.

We are welcomed by a little Mechanical Dog Shaped Vacuum Cleaner that's running around the shop vacuuming the floor.

It works with batteries, and it seems gifted with a life of his own: it bangs against the wall, it turns, it crashes against into something else and so on, until it turns twenty thousand times around the room.

Among the shelves there's something that catches our attention; we look at it in disbelief: it's an electronic Alarm Clock.

~270~

Angry Waiters   *Federico Fumagalli*

What we find appealing is its special function of recording a message to wake you up, instead of the usual alarm ringtone.

We are too tempted to resist, we absolutely want to try this magical technology without asking permission although the big sign 'DON'T TOUCH!' stands in front of us.

After pressing a few buttons at random (no instructions available), we record our message and set the time for the following minute. We don't even bother to check the volume level, so small is the machine.

After sixty long seconds the super-powerful speakers burst up: "WAKE UP, LAZY MOTHERFUCKER! WAKE UP!"

Surprised by the unexpected power, we open our eyes very wide: the message is so loud it could be heard in Fort Lauderdale. We'd like to keep our laughter down, but we simply can't, it's too hard, we burst out laughing really loud, hiding among the shelves with the clock still screaming "WAKE UP, LAZY MOTHERFUCKER! WAKE UP!"

I want to close myself in a drawer, so much I'm laughing, but not even Luca seems intentioned to stop. Each time we look at each other's faces, we carry on laughing like idiots, the message's echo still rumbling around the shop.

Someone is coming to stop the noise and to look for the two stupid idiots who provoked it, despite the clear

~271~

Angry Waiters   *Federico Fumagalli*

invitation not to touch anything.

I put some chocolate in my mouth, trying to stop laughing, but I can't make it and I spit the chocolate on the floor. Luca finds this even funnier, but we'll be in trouble with security very soon if we don't get out.

We move between the shelves towards the exit, and I want to be really silent and really careful to avoid giving away my position, but... on my way out I don't realise the Dangerous Obstacle and under my feet I hear a worryingly 'CRACK!'

I can't believe it. Luca's laughter is now thunder-level; he now has all his hands in his mouth to shut it up, but he can't. I crushed the Hovering Dog, which now doesn't bark any more.

Despite our limited brainpower, we manage to get the hell out of there without getting caught. We run down in the car park, we call another taxi ASAP and we get back to our beloved Golden Princess, with a little relief.

But there is another surprise that takes our relief away: there are the *Time Windows*. It's a shame, because it's already 16.00 and we have to be on duty at 16.30.

Other people around us are protesting.

There's no way of explaining to our supervisors about the Time Windows here, the taxi driver there, bitches here and their sisters there: they don't care about the *reason:* you are late. That's it. You must be punished, carnally if necessary.

Angry Waiters *Federico Fumagalli*

One day a guy fell asleep on the beach; when he woke up, the ship was already gone. One week later the ship came back to the same island: did he get on board? No, my friend: he saw his luggage been thrown down at him, and... Ciao Ciao, Bello! Go back home now!

If someone gets disembarked for a serious reason, he has to manage his trip back home by himself, with his own money – unless the Crew Office hasn't lost it.

~~34~~
USPH: We are under attack

It's my last week.

YYEEEEAAAAHH!!!!!!!

☺☺☺☺☺☺☺☺!!!!

I get the hell out of here!

I-GO-BACK-HOME!

These are the four syllables that I constantly repeat to my work*mates*.

Each passing day, is one day less.

The Final Countdown.

– Seven! – Six! – Five! – Four!...

Down with the Italian mafia! I have had enough of being looked down on by all my foreign work*mates just because I'm Italian!*

I have had enough of being told that if I'm Italian I will make a career quicker *just because I'm Italian!*

I have had enough of people getting grumpy at me *just because I'm Italian!*

I have had enough of being among Italians who get promoted in a couple of contracts over all the workers who have been on board for four or five contracts and they are still one level below them, *just because they are Italian!*

I have had enough of Lobster Nights; Free Sundaes from 15.00 to 16.00; work*mates* who steal 24/7; fighting for a glass or a coffee cup; warnings for peanut pastries; telling-offs for ice creams; white papers taken

Angry Waiters *Federico Fumagalli*

from the docket pad with the *strap-on* it; paying for the Teatime duty in order to sleep less than an hour; skipped lunches and lost dinners; Passengers; working even if I'm sick otherwise I don't get paid; kilometric queues to pile up willing-to-fall plates on clean trays; vanishing breadbaskets; disappearing water jugs; insufficient coffee cups for every Passenger at my station; Passengers; thousands of daily *thank yous* and *you're welcomes*; absurd Bow Drills and dangerous Inductions; Time Windows; sanitising and Galley Rounds; Passengers…

I've had enough of it all.

But: Hey! There's still *one more week*. ☺

On my last week I'm in Lido Lunch shift: at least I don't start too early, though I have to face the forced tour morning-afternoon-evening-night.

My last Galley Round!

Finally during this last week we have the super-unnerving '*Inspection*' by the aliens of the USPH, who check in every corner.

Our Head Waiter warns us: "Make sure you're wearing clean underwear, because they check *everywhere!*"

More or less the inspection works this way:

They board without warning, while we are in deep brata serving Passengers: as soon as the Supervisors realise the intrusion and spread the word, it seems like time suddenly stands still. Time stops. My G-Shock

Angry Waiters   *Federico Fumagalli*

stops too.

Nobody breathes.

Nobody speaks.

Nobody litters.

Nobody moves.

Nobody farts.

Only Passengers complain because they don't receive their food. Supervisors forbid us to serve anything for a while.

There is the *Inspection*.

The *Inspectors* are on board.

Everybody holds their breath.

Everybody with eyes wide shut.

Everybody with ass tightly closed.

Everybody waiting for the final verdict.

Everybody… except for me.

I'm not among them.

I will remember for a long time to come the flavour and the taste of these two pastries I'm holding in my hands: Mr Peanuts Pastry and Lady Strawberry Tartlet, which I'm slowly and deliberately munching side by side.

While everybody is flapping big time up there in the Horizon Court, I'm locked inside the Crew Mess toilet, my mouth busy tasting these delicacies that I have stolen a few minutes earlier from the kitchen fridge, opening the lock with my wine opener.

Sweet revenge…

Mmm… the chocolate covering the peanuts… To the

Angry Waiters   *Federico Fumagalli*

Inspector's face!

MMmm… the strawberry jelly… in the ass of USPH…

MMMMmmmm…the crunchy base of my tartlet… Hey Austrian F&B tall and bald with no more mobile phone: come and get me another *Warning!* MMMMMmmm… the cream of my pastries… a bite for each little bastard I've been fighting with!!

MMMMmmmm…

Knock, Knock!

Eh?

KNOCK, KNOCK!

"Uhmm… Yes?" I ask.

"Inspection! Open the door, please!"

Fuck.

"Vaffanculo! Just a moment!" I reply from inside.

Maybe I should let them crash the door…

KNOCK, KNOCK, KNOCK!!!!

Who cares…?

I swallow my pastries, I flush the water just for the noise, and I wash my hands. I open the door and exit the toilet.

"Sorry!" I apologise to the inspector, who looks at me as if I should know I shouldn't stay in the bathroom during inspections. It's not that I didn't know; I knew it, but as I said… who cares? It's my last week. The week of revenge.

I take the lift and crawl up to the buffet, where I find all my colleagues turned into statues; the Inspectors are

~277~

Angry Waiters *Federico Fumagalli*

in the Washing Area to check with gamma rays any trace of virus, families of bacteria, engaged protozoa and single staphylococcus. They don't find any anomalies, except for a nuclear bomb ready to explode – but clean – and we are all safe.

End of the terrifying inspection.

I'd like to know: what the hell have they checked? Mystery.

So: this last week I'm on Lido Lunch shift: am I allowed to do a Galley Round a little bit more relaxed? Of course not.

Why not?! We were promised some relaxation after the inspection, at least for this last week... but of course not. Never trust a waiter's word, trust me.

Let alone that, I remember that this is the last time for everything! Whatever I do, it's for the last time!

But especially this is the week where anything can happen, especially what you don't expect, when you less expect it.

~~35~~
THE BEAUTY IN RED

I'm on duty with this gay Waiter – Baptista – until the end of my cruise, and during the Champagne Waterfall night I really have the confirmation that for him *pussy* is something *outrageous;* he doesn't want to have anything to do with it, while me, on the other hand, I wouldn't mind a free sample sometimes.

There is this truly pretty lady, in her early thirties, who comes to eat at our station every night. Obviously she likes Baptista.

She tries every possible effort to make him understand that she is not going to leave this ship until she had spent a night with him, but he has something else in his mind. He simply doesn't get it, or if he does, he's a master of disguise.

I like her a lot, she's really hot, and since Baptista is a good guy, I decide to help him. For him this lady is just an annoying mosquito, so I become the slipper with which he could squash her. Only… my intention is all but squashing her.

The night of the Champagne Waterfall she wants to show her incredible beauty entering the dining room all dressed up:

– Black Heels;

– Golden bracelet on her right ankle;

– Long and straight blonde hair;

– Long red dress down to her feet, with two wide

Angry Waiters   *Federico Fumagalli*

splits on both sides of her sexy, smooth legs;

– Unbelievable neckline. Her neckline is used as a showcase for her beautiful breasts that everyone should have the chance to massage once in a lifetime. If she was the Mecca of girls, I would be the first Pilgrim.

– Bra is not present. I know because later on, during the farewell pictures, I would give an extra touch to her back with my maniacal hand.

– Innocent panties, which are just an obstacle during foreplay;

– Light and essential make-up. She doesn't really need any, but just for extra touch;

– Sweet eyes and full lips, the kind that make you think straight away about how wonderful one of her *Lord's Prayers* would be.

She's so beautiful, especially because she doesn't look like a whore.

As soon as she comes to my station, my cock goes crazy and starts to pull in every direction. The whole dining room falls silent, until all you can hear is the men's chorus "WOOAAHH".

When she sits, showing a glimpse of flesh behind the split in her sexy dress, my cock screams to me: '*Attack!*' but my face blushes more than her red dress, because I have to open her triangl… no, no! I have to open the napkin on her triangl… no! I'm getting confused… I have to open the napkin in a triangle shape on her legs, and it's not easy to remain

Angry Waiters   *Federico Fumagalli*

indifferent when I am thirty centimetres away from her boobs. During this operation my head is at her nipples level and I'm about to faint.

She is, anyway, intentioned to conduct the game of seduction with Baptista, who is now recommending *every item* on the menu, as he always does. The only ugly thing of this woman is her mother, who sits next to her and for this occasion she has dressed up like a witch. She's so ugly that if I look at her, I feel like life is not so bad after all.

Baptista suddenly walks in the galley, and I take the chance to serve water from my full water jugs to the Beauty and the Beast. Baptista hasn't noticed that the Beauty has made herself so pretty just for him, but who blames him? He is gay, what to do?

The Beauty asks me something about him, and I must confess: "Excuse me, I understand your intentions, but you see: my Waiter is gay. He doesn't even notice young ladies like yourself." And I make a ☹ face.

The Beast screams in disconcert: "Oh No! Really?! How about you?!"

I look at her, then I look at the Beauty:

"Eh no, madam: I like women!"

"Well done, you boy, but I'm surprised." Carries on the mother.

"Surprised about what?"

"That you like women. You don't look straight at all."

"AH really?" I ask, a bit annoyed.

Angry Waiters   *Federico Fumagalli*

"Yea, you look very... feminine."

"Very feminine? Fantastic."

"Where are you from?"

"I'm from Italy."

"Ah! Italiano! *Buenas tarde!*"

"You fucking kidding me..." I think, putting a hand on my face.

But then I must carry on with the hammering service.

When this torture ends up (torture because it's not so easy to get my mind together when I'm so close to somebody that stirs inside me the most erotic fantasies), at the end of the service the Beauty and the Beast want to take the farewell pictures: first I take one to them together with Baptista, with him standing in the middle, his hands in the front keeping the position and the typical expression like "I'm not going to touch you, *you women!*"

Then it's my turn: I move in between them, watching Baptista holding the camera; I'm busy trying not to touch the Beast's wrinkly skin on my left, while my right hand is having a panoramic tour around the Beauty's back in order to find the right point for the hug. Starting from the shoulder I reach down almost to her butt – perfect butt that speaks by itself: *'Don't forget abutt me!'*

Touching her back, I get confirmation that a bra didn't find place on her body.

And there it happens…

The unbelievable happens…

~282~

Angry Waiters   *Federico Fumagalli*

Ending of the photos, the Beast all happy runs to Baptista for congratulations and tips and various bullshit about the Excellent service; in the same moment the Beauty in Red leans down (she's much taller than me) reaching my ear level and whispers to me: "See you later at the Champagne Waterfall; and by the way my cabin is D317... I wish after midnight you might want to come up to say farewell..." and she blinks at me, walking away.

I freeze.

I look at her ass dancing left and right, until she walks out of the doors, while my cock is having a wrestling fight with my underwear to rush out and reach the Beauty and reassure her butt: *'No, I won't forget abutt you!'*

The Champagne Waterfall comes, my head is already somewhere else. My thoughts are already at the end of it. I don't care of warnings any more: they can catch me while walking out of her cabin after we *farewelled* each other properly, getting charged, disembarked... I don't care any more.

It's my last week! I get off anyway! Nobody can stop me! It's time for payback.

I meet her on Deck 7 during the Champagne Waterfall, while fooling around in the ballrooms with my giant tray full of pastries which, one by one, become the dinner I didn't have. Who cares about hiding? Passengers ask me: "Hey Fredrico, what does this green and pink pastry, the last one on your tray,

~283~

tastes like?"

I look at it: I grin. Those morons called me again with a wrong name. They look at me in disbelief while I put the pastry in my mouth, chewing it and announcing that... "Mmm... it tastes like a mix of apple and strawberry! Oh... no more? Don't worry *mate,* I'm going to get you some more."

Then I spot her again; her long red dress covers the whole length of her body, but the opening at the sides let me see her legs. I take in a big lungful of air, walking toward her. Probably I'm blushing big time, I feel my face burning. When I'm close enough she points to her clock, I point to my cock, and I nod, positively looking. She ☺s at me, whispering one more time that after midnight, at any time, she is alone in her cabin waiting for me. "*As if I could forget abutt you…*"

So, this is it: I've heard her with my ears, I saw her with my eyes and I touched her with my hands, so she really exists! She's not a hallucination and she's not a dream! She's not fake! I'm not dreaming! Never felt so alive!

I almost want to throw this stupid tray into the crowd and climb up to her cabin, but I don't want to do anything stupid: I want to avoid getting caught *before* I've had sex. That would be really embarrassing.

I look at her one last time, until she enters the lift. I'm fainting. She's going up. And soon I will be up with her with the best of my pastries: My Banana Flambé! I can't believe it!

Angry Waiters   *Federico Fumagalli*

I'm getting too excited.

I find it hard to keep calm and carry on, but I reveal for the first time my most sincere ☺☺☺☺☺☺☺☺☺☺☺☺☺☺☺s to everybody, even to my most hated work*mates,* to Head Waiters, Supervisors. I even smile sincerely to Passengers.

Time passes slowly, but passes anyway, and when 01.00 comes…

My pressure intensifies: ready to run. The Head Waiter is making the last roll call: "Mihai, Ciprian, Raszvan, Robert S., Tomasz, Robert M., the other Tomasz, Dorian, Tancula, Frenderico, Sukan, Anchana, Ramil, Aneta… OK: now you can go and see you tomorr…"

GO!

The Head Waiter hasn't finished the sentence that I'm already out of the ballroom. I'm faster than light, crossing the corridor of the ship to arrive in my cabin entering from the keyhole; I take shower without even getting undressed, kicking the Thai gay out of the bathroom; I dry myself up with few pirouettes, I change my clothes with the power of my thought, and I smash the door down to exit because I have the power of the dragon inside me. I sprint like a rocket toward the lifts of the Crew Mess. Hey Austrian F&B: where are you now?!?

I go up a few floors, then I exit to take the Passenger lift, being careful not to be caught *now,* not *before* I slept with one of the most beautiful ladies I've ever seen. I reach the area with the four lifts, two in front of each one, choosing the one on the right.

I check my pockets: condoms? Don't have any. This was an unplanned event. But who cares?

And by the way something tells me she must have some for sure, maybe with the DOTQCIG logo on them: "S-Crew Me!"

I point my finger to the keypad: I'm sweating.

'So… This is it!'

I ☺ again.

My eyes are scanning the floor's panel, shining gold, optimism in my whole body.

D329…

No.

That was C547…

No.

A261…

E308…

No…

Wait a moment...

F135…

B243…

…no…

… what was that...?

H819...?

G747...?

My fingers move like crazy tentacles over the buttons…

My mind engages a battle against my memory…

"Think! Think! Think! Think for fuck's sake!"

M987...

"Keep calm and remember her cabin number!"

T651...

"Come on! Come on! Come on! You can do it! You can do it!"

J392...

U646...

No... this is not possible...

"Remember! Remember! Remember! Neurons, do your job! Brain, help me out! I've never asked you anything before, but now I need you! Do not abandon me! Don't leave me!"

K911...

R118...

Y007...

P45...

...I can't believe it...

...I don't want this to be true...

...please tell me it's not true...

...it's really true...

...it's sadly true...

...but it shouldn't be true...

I close my eyes, cursing the hell out of me; I call out for Gods who bark, Goddesses who moo, Sons of the Creator, failed Saviours of mankind, Virgin and not Virgin Marys, Nativity scenes catching fire, Three Wise Men sodomised by their camels, piggy Deities, Prophets who go to the mountain but then the mountain crumbles down, orgies of Saints and Martyrs...

...I forgot...

...I forgot her...

"I forgot her cabin number?!"

I forgot her cabin number?

Fuck... Yes!

I forgot her bloody ca-bin-num-ber!!

How is that possible?!?

The world sinks under my feet.

M643...

A271...

No...

I never felt so useless.

My cock shrinks.

My best friend Alessio would tell me:

"You are an insult to mankind!"

My best friend Mauro would tell me:

"You are the prick made person!"

And I must agree…

☹

~~36~~
LAST DAY

The day of general disembarkation I have to work very early in the morning. At 05.15 I'm on duty, half an hour earlier than usual, still furious with myself for the missed chance to have sex with the Beauty in Red, the Goddess of Erotic Dreams.

Exploited, squeezed till the last minute.

I'm in Fort Lauderdale, on a Lido Breakfast shift at the Horizon Court; we work only inside the buffet, without using the wide spaces outside the deck because it's raining like hell, under an unbelievable slaughtering chaos due to lack of space. Passengers don't move out of our way even under intimidation, seats are lacking but they *pretend* to be seated anyway, even if there's no space. They *demand* to be seated, not understanding and not listening to what we are telling them. I tell them: "*On that way!*" with the promise that *on the other side* they will have a table, just ask one of our friendly Head Waiters that will be more than happy to help you (Maybe. But I had to get rid of them). First of all, the Head Waiters are indecently devastated by the chaotic situation, plus there is *me* sending *everybody* to them. Soon the other side becomes fully crowded with angry buffalo that will soon start to complain about anything possible, until the last moment available to cancel our tips. All they want is a seat: hey Head Waiters! Give 'em a seat! They paid for

Angry Waiters Federico Fumagalli

it! They *must* have a bloody seat! Come on! Sort it out!

The problem is that the seats are available, but Passengers don't want to share a table if there is someone else already sitting on it. One table, six seats, three people. Three other seats are taken by bags and rucksacks.

I keep an eye on my other disembarking colleagues: when they disappear, I do too.

Fifteen minutes later Robert S. tells me that he has had enough of being here, and he is going to have his own breakfast in the Crew Mess. I follow him.

"Did the Head Waiter allow you to go for breakfast?" I ask.

"With this brata? Absolutely *not*."

"Alright! Let's go!"

We leave the buffet without notifying any Supervisor or Head Waiter, leaving this chaos to them. They are overpaid for it, so let them get on with it. My stomach is rumbling big time. Why do we have to work forty-five minutes in the morning if we have to disembark early? Because the managers are sadist and like to see us suffering.

After our breakfast (Robert and I weren't the only ones to have left the buffet: we were only the last ones! At least twenty unauthorised Junior Waiters were already eating in the Crew Mess, and now I understand why the shit hit the dozen fans on the buffet: nobody was working. Only Head Waiters and Supervisors. Everyone was hiding).

Angry Waiters Federico Fumagalli

We need to change our uniform, so I get back to my cabin, take off my Jungle uniform I used for the buffet, I put on the white one I use in the dining room, then I go to Canaletto for the meeting.

Meeting? What for?! And why with our uniform if we don't have to serve anybody?

Half an hour passes by, nothing happens and nobody comes to tell us anything, but then the speakers switch on and a mysterious voice announces that we can all go to hell for the last time.

Somebody comes to tell us that we can *finally* go to consume our breakfast, and we all get astonished; the question in our minds is: does anyone have an idea of what to do?

Seems like NO.

We all make a second breakfast in an hour, then we go back to our cabins to change our clothes, civilian ones this time. Because of heat, chaos and humidity I am already sweating, so I decide to take my last shower in the mignon bathroom. I get undressed, I put all my underwear in a plastic bag that I put inside my luggage, I close the luggage with the lock and I wash myself.

When I exit the shower I need of course to dress up but I realise that I don't have any more clean underpants. What do I do? Do I reopen the luggage and take the dirty underpants from the plastic bag? Mmm... not really keen on doing that.

So, the only option is to wear my trousers without underpants. Nobody would notice. Not Aneta, not

~291~

Angry Waiters   *Federico Fumagalli*

Agata, not the Beauty in Red, not Baptista. I just need to be careful not to scratch my balls against the zip.

Just another little inconvenience.

This sorted out, I go back to Canaletto where earlier on we were just told to get out.

This time there is somebody: one of the Head Waiters who has just jumped down from the buffet looks at us very angrily; he has been fighting the battle to the last croissant.

He starts with a general ronzata: "What the fuck! You all just disappeared! We were slammed and tortured! Fucking Passengers complaining and shouting! Everything was missing! It was the worse thing I've ever witnessed! I can't even tell you not to do it next time because you are leaving, and I'm honestly envious! And to finish…" his face becomes a big ☺ing grin: "… I can't even blame you for what you did because I did it myself many times when I was in your miserable position, so… Congratulations for your *excellent job*, *inventive, effort, whatsoever…* and now go to collect your luggage, get the hell out of here and *fuck off* as much as you can! I don't want to see you any more! GO! GO! GO!"

We clap our hands and we wait in turn to receive our references, our money, to hand back our Laminex and the key cards.

We are explained what to do for our disembarkation (if it was for me, I would just collect my belongings and walk out without looking back).

Angry Waiters   *Federico Fumagalli*

Next appointment is in Bernini for another meeting. OH COME ON!!! LET US GET OFF HERE! We could have got up two hours later!

But there we go: slowly the dining room fills up with waiting-for-disembarkation people. When enough time has passed and our words are getting dangerous, the fat lady from the Crew Office comes to make the final roll call. This is a long one, because it's three hundred of us: 'This is SPARTAAA!' I want to scream, and kick her in the pit. She is the same lady that did not manage to send my money into my bank account.

We have to proceed toward the gangway to collect our luggage that has been *accurately checked to avoid theft*.

We placed our luggage there earlier on, between one meeting and another.

Theft?

Oh no…

My heart stops beating again. It happened many times lately.

I have stolen…

…but I have been very smart… maybe they haven't realised it…

When I arrive to the gangway I find out that our bags are not there, with an inspector ready to give them back to us on presentation of our ID: our bags are literally *out of the ship*, inside big containers, all piled up like pyramids, under the heaviest rain the US has ever faced

Angry Waiters   Federico Fumagalli

in history. Raindrops are as big as bathtubs, incessantly falling down without mercy.

I find a lifebelt and go get the bags. After I got them, I reach the bus that will bring us to the airport. I get inside and I sit among my Italian colleagues, assembling the loudest tribe in the middle of the bus. We spend the trip doing burping competitions, curse crosswords, sexual verdicts and thundering wild screams.

I just feel weird and uncomfortable without underpants.

The driver drives us to Miami airport as fast as ever to get rid of us ASAP.

Once in the airport we notice the very long queue that is waiting for us; for this reason we divide into tribes, with the only intention of spreading terror among the people that obviously can't understand the meaning of our noisy head banging.

I buy another CD player for my sister (the one she borrowed to me, I destroyed), I call home to alert the nation that I'm coming back, I eat in a fast food the greasiest and fattiest food ever, and together with my tribe I reach the Check In area where we entertain the people with our freedom anthems.

While I proceed with serenity in my soul, my mind alerts me that everything is going too smoothly… everything it's OK, everything's fine…

It's time to worry.

Worry about what?

Angry Waiters   *Federico Fumagalli*

I don't know, I've been careful enough, I don't possess drugs, weapons... my documents are OK, passport in my pocket...

OK. Proceed.

First I need to face the Metal Detector: I also have to take my shoes off, which contain some metallic parts. Then I take my watch off.

I walk through.

BIIIIPP!

What the hell?! Oh, yeah, my necklace.

Take it off.

Pass through again.

BIIIIPP!

'What now?' I think.

My belt! How stupid...

Take it off.

The security staff are staring at me.

He motions me to come forward again.

BIIIIPP!!

"What's wrong?!?" I say, looking down, left and right.

The agent stops me and comes close to me with two handheld metal detectors. He swings them around me, and they blip again.

"There is something in your trousers. Take it out."

"No, there's nothing. I emptied all my pockets."

"Then, there must be something hidden in the inside pockets. Do you have inside pockets?"

"No, I don't. I swear."

Angry Waiters   *Federico Fumagalli*

"You should come in the office and take your trousers off, just a security procedure."

"Whaaaat?!?" my mind screams. *"No way!"*

"Are you sure this is necessary?" I ask.

Shit, I'm not wearing underpants!

"It's a necessary precaution. If you have nothing to hide, then you shouldn't be afraid."

"No, no, no! That's not a good idea at all! I can't take my trousers off!" I say to myself. *"Please don't let this happen! You don't want to see this!"*

In the meanwhile, one of his colleagues calls him, indicating my bag.

Another security guard is pointing at me.

I'm fucked.

I'm sure they found out that I took away all the uniforms I used for months.

I'm just worried about all the people that might look at me while explaining to the guard what I've done and why. I couldn't bear it.

The guard is ravaging through my hand luggage. Suddenly I remember that my uniforms are not there: they are in the other luggage, the one I will collect in Milan; the one that has been *accurately inspected to avoid theft*.

The guard picks up something from my bag:

"What's this?"

"It's a wine opener!"

Has he ever seen one?

"I know what this is! But tell me why are you keeping

Angry Waiters   *Federico Fumagalli*

it in your hand luggage?!"

"Because I'm a waiter and I just finished duty and I had no chance to put it in my other luggage…"

"You can't keep this with you on board, it's against safety rules, do you understand? Now this is under requisition."

I can hardly swallow: my wine opener is holy for me! I never go anywhere without it! But I can't discuss with him, I'm so close to getting away from here…

"OK, I'm sorry…"

"You can go now. Have a nice flight."

"I wish your family flu and runny nose…"

The other security guy (the one who wanted me to take my trousers off in his office) suddenly forgets about me and goes back to scan other passengers.

I let out a huge breath of healthy relief: I don't need to show him my little friend.

But I lost my wine opener. It was a gift from a friend.

I carry on walking sadly until the waiting room, it's so far away that I could arrive to Milan by walking, I order a tea, wait for the airplane to come, get on it, sit on my very uncomfortable seat in middle row and I fasten my seatbelt.

I breathe relieved.

I look at the hostesses, one prettier than the others.

The Captain inserts the key and switches on the engines.

Their noise reminds me of my car.

He pulls the gearstick backward and presses the

Angry Waiters   *Federico Fumagalli*

pedal.

The aircraft moves.

I think that one day I'll have to come back on the ship to collect the giant stereo that I certainly could not take with me.

Aircraft standing on the runway.

Engines running wildly.

My mind running too.

I wait to switch my CD player on, when I'll be high in the sky, like near the moon.

I feel the pressure pushing on my back due to the aircraft's sudden movement.

I look at the landscape that's running backward.

The aircraft reaches the necessary speed and raises up, flying away from Miami, thundering outrageously.

I really made it, and I ☺…

… And...

… and...

HEY!

No…!

Wait...

Wait a moment…!

It's just in this moment that it comes to my mind…

…Wait…

…I remember…

… I remember it!!

Yes! Yes!

I remember! I remember it!

D...

D317...

It's the…

It's her...

It's her number...

It's her cabin number…

It's the cabin number of the Beauty in Red!

… "STOP THIS FUCKING AIRPLAAAAAAANE!!!"

~~37~~
EPILOGUE

In an isolated island floating in the Philippine Sea, an old and bald fisherman who had seen everything in his life was rowing his bamboo canoe to get back to shore.

It had been a brilliant sunny day, calm and not so windy, and the sun still had a few hours before setting.

The man crossed over the last coral reef of the quiet lagoon, observing with tired eyes the white sandy bottom through the crystalline water. Some multicolour fish swam under him, as if they were suspended in mid-air, giving life to an underwater dance between corals.

Once arriving on the sand, the old and bald man got off his canoe, he dragged it onto solid ground and tied it up to the usual wooden hook with a strong rope. He looked around, almost blinded by the shining sand of that exotic beach, surrounded by palm trees and bungalows, one of which was the one he lived in. He then greeted a woman stretched out on her hammock and he entered his bungalow, holding on his shoulder the net containing the big fish he caught that day.

He pulled the fish out, leaning on the table to clean it: he washed it, cut it, took out its bones, and then he had the intention to cook it for dinner.

As he put his hands inside the fish's belly, he felt something strange; it was something hard, something that shouldn't have been there: after a few seconds of delicate work with his cutting knife he managed to extract the out-of-place object.

Once the blood and the guts were washed away, the old and bald man found himself holding a grey mobile phone, without antenna, still switched on. On the blue display a small envelope was blinking, indicating the presence of a text message.

"Ito ang kauna-unahang pagkakataon…" (That's the first time ever…) he murmured, not believing what was in front of his eyes.

Curious, he pressed a button to read the message:

'You are gonna die in 10, 9, 8, 7, 6…!'

~~38~~

GLOSSARY

(In no particular order)

RUMENTA: asshole; referred to colleagues and Passengers without distinction of sex, skin colour, nationality, salary, celery, religious problems, age, education, ignorance, level of *inglisch*, mental issues, muscle pains, migraine, nausea.

Origin: Romania.

CIPPETTONE: Passenger who doesn't leave tips.

It doesn't matter how good you are and how excellent your service might be: HIS wallet is sealed and his pockets empty.

Easy to recognise because, due to his very short arms, he looks like a deformed mini T. rex.

Origin: Italo-American (Cheap + Pettone).

RONZATA: telling off, scolding. It's usually delivered by any superior, when you least expect it, even if is it's not your fault. *Especially* when it's not your fault.

Origin: unknown.

BRATA: Shit.

In waiting jargon, when there is too much work, there are too many Passengers, and you have too much to do.

Angry Waiters   *Federico Fumagalli*

You just can't manage it any more; then, you are surrounded by brata.

Origin: on board, but very much used in Tuscany.

CARAMELLA: last minute table of latecomers.

Dining room and kitchen close in two minutes.

You are tired.

All you want is to finish and go back to your cabin to sleep.

But someone comes in on an empty stomach and the Head Waiter sits them at your station?

Congratulations: you just got a caramella.

You now hate both the Passenger and the Head Waiter.

Origin: on board (although in Italian it means "candy").

STATION: aka service station. Not to be confused with Petrol Station.

Working area where the waiters keep plates, side plates, silverware, coffee cups, coffee pots, hand grenades, big black box and small black box.

COMPLAINT: something is wrong.

If after a lightning there is thunder, after a complaint there is a Tips Cancellation.

Origin: in the Passenger's brain.

JUNIOR WAITER: runner, commis de rang, bus

Angry Waiters *Federico Fumagalli*

boy, slave.

Main pillar of hospitality; key element of the dining room; magnificence of the pizzeria; emperor of the food industry; saviour of empty stomachs.

Without Junior Waiters orders don't reach those damn food dealers in the kitchen; food doesn't reach hungry Passengers; you don't eat even if you cry; without Junior Waiters you starve to death.

Your table doesn't get cleared and reset; your glass doesn't get wiped with a dirty napkin; your bread roll is not taken with a chlorine flavoured disposable glove; drinks don't walk to your table from the bar; without Junior Waiters you die of thirst.

Underestimated by Passengers and Management, the Junior Waiter is an endangered species on the brink of disappearing; the Junior Waiter is victim of everlasting pranks, eternal fatigue, quick and tired steps, work exploitation, loss of human rights, sleep deprivation, back pain, feet on fire, nutritional blindness, thirst for vengeance, easy swearing, complaints made at his image, unnecessary blaming, miserable tips, buckets of sweat.

Even so, he still manages to wish you a nice meal with a smile on his face.

The Junior Waiter must be respected.

Because the Junior Waiter doesn't forget a face and one day he will be back.

To spit in your meal in another restaurant.

Angry Waiters   *Federico Fumagalli*

WAITER: chef de rang, the one who takes the orders at the station. Without any particular reason earns more than a Junior Waiter.

He is in charge of theoretical duties among which are: thinking about; delegating the Junior Waiter to carry out what has been thought about; entertain Passengers with idiocy, mediocrity, and futility; boasting about his abilities; showing off; insulting the Junior Waiter; arguing with the Junior Waiter; building castles in the air; seeing a glass half empty and asking the Junior Waiter to fill it up; seeking revenge on the Junior Waiter; looking a gift horse in the mouth; hiding the tips of the Junior Waiter; pretending to be busy; cleansing his sins.

If he's not too tired, he shows his horrible calligraphy after taking an order from a Passenger. If the Junior Waiter has a master's degree in Hieroglyphs he carries on, otherwise the Waiter will send him to the Passenger with the claim that he has to learn how to take orders.

SUPERVISOR: the one who supervises. Hybrid beast half Waiter half Head Waiter, delegates Waiters to do what Head Waiters have delegated upon him. Conjugation of the verb: doing fuck all. The Supervisor roams around checking and spying on behalf of Head Waiters.

Semantically speaking, he does not possess superpowers.

HEAD WAITER: aka Maître, boss of the brigade. Mythological creature with the power to disappear when he is needed, you can usually find him hidden in the pantry feeding on meals previously stolen from Junior Waiters.

His very weak physical structure doesn't make him ideal for heavy tasks, but with a bit of luck and patience you may see him performing light work during Island Nights preparing pasta and crêpes in front of Passengers.

When he is not busy giving ronzatas to Junior Waiters, you can observe him in his natural habit – the gym – where he spends long hours sculpting his ego and lifting his eyes on the sexy ladies who are working out (how to avoid him).

F&B MANAGER: aka Food and Beverage Manager, usually shortened to F&B.

The F&B is in charge, but we don't know what of.

Halfway between Head Waiter and Maître d', he is always hanging on your balls ruining your day with ronzatas, orders, you can't do this and you can't do that.

In the Crew Mess he eats in a protected area to find shelter from angry waiters and poisonous food.

Be aware of F&Bs coming from violent and uncivilised countries, like Austria.

If on the first impression he doesn't like you, he will fuck the girl you like. If he doesn't like you even on

Angry Waiters   *Federico Fumagalli*

the second impression, he will fuck *you too*.

Generally speaking, the first impression is good enough.

MAÎTRE D': aka Boss of the Bosses, there is no one like him. In the herd there can only be an alpha waiter.

Even Head Waiters fear him, for he is the only member of the crew with the power of *ronzating* them.

You don't see him often, as he prefers the comfortable sofa in his quiet office.

Promotions usually go through him, but for that to happen he needs to go through you.

CHLORINE: halogen element, heavy, incombustible, soluble in water, is a highly toxic gas for the respiratory apparatus; it's obtained by electrolysis. Deadly gas used in war. Very dangerous and damaging.

For all these reasons it is being given to the Junior Waiter who uses it to sanitise everything, especially items that will come in contact with the Passenger. If used without protection, the Junior Waiter will lose his fingerprints; breathed continuously, will disintegrate the Junior Waiter's lungs.

Nonetheless, chlorine is considered the most powerful weapon to kill viruses and bacteria.

And Junior Waiters.

WARNING: aka don't fucking do that again!

Angry Waiters   *Federico Fumagalli*

Usually for something negative, hits every Junior Waiter without exception. The more the warnings the earlier you get thrown out to sea.

Ironically, often the warning strikes without warning.

GALLEY: technical name of the kitchen area of a ship.

Place of clashes and battles among Junior Waiters and Chefs, here cutlery is washed, dishes are prepared, speed competitions take place, glasses are broken, insolent and innovative adjectives are thrown at Passengers.

PASS: separation border between Chef's working area and Junior Waiter's Labour Camp, is made of long heated shelves with lamps that keep food hot. Estimated temperature: 1000°C.

Without this separation the physical contact between the parties would be unavoidable: slaps, punches and flying kicks that would put Bruce Lee to shame. And there are not enough doctors.

DISHWASHER: task usually undertaken by *friendly* and *hardworking Indians*, the dishwasher is one of the most noble and important jobs of the whole of hospitality industry.

Without dishwashers the Passengers would eat on dirty plates, drink out of smeared cups, lick filthy cutlery, becoming more rumenta, more cippettone, and

~308~

Angry Waiters   *Federico Fumagalli*

place more complaints.

The dishwasher is the main pillar of the on board hygiene and he must wash and dry quickly, efficiently, continuously, excellently, always smiling, and kindly helping people in need.

After the Junior Waiter, the dishwasher is the superstar of the ship, a very respectable element and number one colleague.

Unfortunately, on the DOTQCIG someone forgot to teach these details to those bastards, resulting in utmost hate and despicable behaviour.

If they could stab you in your back, they will surely do it using, of course, a silver knife that you have already polished for the Galley Round.

Then you have to wash it again.

STATION: portion of dining room, number of tables given to the lovely couple, Waiter and Junior Slave.

On the ship the station consists of a maximum of six tables, with a limit of twenty Passengers.

Must be always attended by at least one of the two waiters, with sporadic visits by a Head Waiter, recently awaken from lethargy and looking for hidden food in the station, to be secretly consumed in the pantry.

PASSENGER: person on holiday on board. Paying customer. Main cause of tips cancellation, complaints, headaches, mental stress, genital cancer.

To learn more, read the book all over again.

Angry Waiters   *Federico Fumagalli*

CREW MESS: staff canteen, area for crew feeding. Sometimes managed by a selected chef; all the other times abandoned and left alone to anarchy and mutiny.

When the food is gone, it's gone.

Since meal quality and taste are never proportionally linked, the crew mess is the main reason why floor staff steals food on duty.

The crew mess is also the main point to go to if you want to reach any other part of the ship from your cabin.

INDUCTION: introductory course/courses.

Mini seminars that take you by the throat as soon as you step on board.

Among the few real useful things of the whole cruise, they teach you to survive. They cover hygiene, health, safety, emergency exits, escape routes, firebreak doors, life jackets, organisational skills, team work, fire extinguishers, first aid, lifeboats, and more.

Unfortunately, for unknown reasons, most times during an induction nothing happens (see Bow Drill) and time wasted is seldom appreciated.

BOW DRILL: see nothingness, void, emptiness.

BLUE CARD: document to be taken with you at any induction or drill, it *should* register your presence there.

LIFE JACKET: made of a visible, very bright orange colour, arouses hilarity among your colleagues if you actually wear it on your first induction.

It's also used to keep you floating each time the ship sinks, therefore saving your life.

USPH(S): United States Public Health (Service): similar to European HACCP – just tougher – it's one of the many nightmares that hits you while still awake.

One of the main reasons for Head Waiters to put Junior Waiters under stress.

USPH only operates in USA territory and is feared by everyone, including the Captain.

BUFFET STEWARDS: buffet assistants.

One of the very few positions below the Junior Waiters, this is where the newly embarked worker bees begin their career.

Beginning one position below Junior Waiters on the first cruise fills Buffet Stewards with strong resentment and supreme hate towards Junior Waiters.

As if all the abuses Junior Waiters endure from the people *above* in the pyramid of power weren't enough.

WATER JUGS: holy grail.

Plastic containers of water whose value is inestimable, for it seems that everyone wearing a uniform is always trying to steal one from someone else.

MISE EN PLACE: table setting; to clear the table, change the table cloth, put cutlery, glasses and napkins. Everything on the table that will be used by the Passenger is called *mise en place*.

For unknown reasons, there is an international agreement stating that items already placed on a table *shall not* be stolen.

But of course, being in international waters means that the agreement *shall* be broken.

Origin: France.

BUTTA GIÙ: pronounced *Bootta ju*. Technical jargon that the Waiter shouts to the Junior Waiter, referred to a dish to be served promptly. Literally: the dish does not have to be served quickly; it should be thrown (butta) down (giù) to the Passenger like a frisbee.

Possibly onto his cranium.

Origin: Italy.

SHITDAY: the worst day of your week.

Some weeks shitday is seven days out of seven, so it makes no difference.

GLOVES: latex or disposable gloves.

Theoretically placed in the proper container hung on the wall, accessible to everybody; in practice the

Angry Waiters   *Federico Fumagalli*

container is always empty, except for when the aforementioned container has completely disappeared, a circumstance that makes its fullness or emptiness totally irrelevant.

Originally introduced to hygienically pick up bread from giant baskets and then thrown away, the gloves are ideal to wash your socks in the miserable sink in your cabin. ~~Keep as long as you can.~~ Throw away after first use.

NIGHTWORKERS: aka nightworkers.

Lazy bastards who spend their time sleeping where the CCTV can't see them, they finish their shift tired leaving all the brata for you to clean and set up.

Some of them have sex in the dining room leaving condoms on the floor. Who cares? It's the Junior Waiter's task to clean up.

STARBOARD SIDE: main cause of headaches and mental instability, for no one has yet understood its location.

Some say on the righthand side of the ship.

PORT SIDE: main cause of dental pain and a sore throat, for no one knows where to find it.

Some say on the lefthand side of the ship.

CHURCH: Place of prayer and worship, where genuflection is performed for more than one purpose.

Angry Waiters   *Federico Fumagalli*

The tithes (offerings) are quite expensive, but at least the sermon is not boring, being made of just a few words most of which are repeated and easy to remember.

Sins are not forgiven: they are requested and accomplished.

The host (holy bread) has various sizes and is mostly taken by mouth, but not only there.

If you pray without protection only a miracle will save you from a venereal disease.

GANGWAY: authorised way out for the crew.
Not to be mistaken with GANGBANG.

ALWAYS AVAILABLE: tattooed on Agata's forehead, it is also a kitchen section where the menu never changes.

From there you can always pick up the same dishes because, as you can see, they are always available: grilled salmon, steak, fettuccine Alfredo.

Introduced to compensate the problem of choice for difficult Passengers, it's easy to reach once you have mastered its location.

Difficult to pronounce for Italians, it sounds like this: *olueis aveilebol.*

ELEVATOR: American for lift.
Origin: Aerosmith (love in an Elevator).

~314~

Angry Waiters   *Federico Fumagalli*

SUNNY SIDE UP EGGS: English for "Ox's eye style eggs" in Italian.

DUDEN PIZTA MUOTTI: go back into your mother's pussy, back where you came from.
Origin: Romania.

SUGI PULA: one of the areas of Agata's awards and expertise, means *suck my dick, give me a blowjob*.
Origin: Romania.

PANTRY: storeroom.
Small room used as a store to stock cleaning products or canned food, it's usually occupied by a Head Waiter who is secretly eating.
While on duty.
Food stolen from a Junior Waiter.

SILVER PASTE: product used to polish every item made of silver, there is never enough of it for everybody.
It provokes resentments toward colleagues, fights and wrestling matches in the galleys.

SEXUAL HARASSMENT: nobody comes to offer this to you, but if you attempt it, even slightly, it rains brata on you and there are no umbrellas around.

SLOW SERVICE: it doesn't matter how quick you

Angry Waiters   *Federico Fumagalli*

run: for the Passenger you could have been quicker.
No tips.

NAME BADGE: states your name.
Incorrectly.

DAY OFF: unknown event that never takes place for the whole duration of the contract.

SICK DAY: fasten your belt and brace yourself to work anyway.
There is no such thing like staying in bed if you feel unwell.
You chopped off a whole finger? You cracked a knee? Heavy headache, nausea, vomit, dizziness, stomach cramps, lungs filled with concrete, smashed your teeth, erratic erections, tongue stuck on ice, fainting, respiratory issues, cardiac arrest? Get yourself a fucking aspirin and BE on duty!
Your monthly period is so strong you are bleeding out of every orifice? Plug them and run to your goddamn dining room.
NOW!
Because if you don't work, you are not paid.

DOBRANOC: goodnight in Polish.
Origin: Sweden.
No, of course not: Poland.

~316~

Angry Waiters   *Federico Fumagalli*

INSPECTION: main cause of heart failure and farts in 3D.

It can occur at any (un)given moment and without warning, but only in USA territory, so if you are smart you kind of know when you should expect it.

The USPHS staff checks sanitary and hygiene level of every spot and hole on the ship. They are very kinky, as they check literally *everywhere*, every spot, every hole, even yours: reason why it is advisable to wear clean underpants.

WINDOWS: a barrier of thirty minutes time frame during which no one is allowed in or out of the ship. It happens at random, but mostly when you need to get back on board after your break.

If you are late to start your shift, you'll be even later.

Expect a nice ronzata from your head of department.

SIDE JOBS: extra duties to be performed during the week which allow you to have off Saturday mornings and afternoons.

You might marvel at why Agata never works on Saturdays: it's because of the quality of her side jobs.

These side jobs consist of: counting dirty table cloths and napkins; extra cleaning; stock taking, and other tasks that nobody wants or has time to do.

Having never voluntarily taken part in any of these side jobs, one time, as a punishment, someone from Austria appoints me to take charge of cleaning the

Coffee machine filters of Mr Caffettiere, together with him.

Mr Caffettiere is not so excited about it, since we are not on best friend terms: once I dropped three of his monumentally extraordinary café lattes and he refused to make them again on the *grounds* that I would drop them again – as if I would do it intentionally, so he arrives very late just to annoy me.

Taken by a monumentally extraordinary thirst, I find an unfindable glass tumbler and, before topping it up with ice tea, I chuck it in the monumental ice machine instead of using the proper plastic scoop.

Result number A: the tumbler shatters amongst the ice cubes, disintegrating into thousands of fragments.

Result number B: (now I can laugh about it, but at that time I DID NOT laugh about it; not during the monumentally extraordinary ronzata I received, not during the extenuating process of cleaning the whole ice machine)... Of course I can't just pick up the biggest shards: I have to melt all of the ice, and when we are talking of about 300kg of ice there's not much to laugh about.

Then, I have to rinse the container, cleaning it super carefully, ask a Head Waiter to check it (disturbing him while eating in the pantry), if it's not excellent enough, repeat the whole process again and switch the machine on to remake the ice and leaving tens and tens of Junior Waiters in full brata because to make 300kg of ice cubes it takes... ice ages; they all hate me, but who cares? I hate them too.

Lesson learned.

But… what was that?

Angry Waiters   *Federico Fumagalli*

Daughter Of The Queen Coloured In Gold (DOTQCIG) Cruise Ship

Three ways to hide from dangerous Supervisors:

one

Angry Waiters *Federico Fumagalli*

two

three

Printed in Poland
by Amazon Fulfillment
Poland Sp. z o.o., Wrocław